ESSAYS ON

ROBERT BROWNING

BY

MARION LITTLE

LONDON:
SWAN SONNENSCHEIN & CO., LIM.
PATERNOSTER SQUARE
1899

CONTENTS.

BROWNING'S PUBLIC.

MOST of us know Tennyson's own account of his reading of Browning's *Sordello*; how there were only two lines in it that he understood, and neither of them was true; they were the opening and the closing lines:—
"*Who will may hear Sordello's story told*," and "*Who would has heard Sordello's story told*"! Even the most devoted reader of Browning's poetry must laugh over this story with that sympathetic laughter which betrays that something not very unlike this has happened to him too, not once, as in the reading of Sordello, which of course is a by-word, but many times. A similar experience causes the majority of readers to resolve forthwith that they will not read anything

B

written by the same poet again. This, in fact, was the attitude of the reading public as a whole towards Browning's poetry for a great number of years, and is that of a large section of it to-day,—the attitude of those who have neither leisure nor patience, nor indeed inclination, to face a stubborn study ; and who, in giving Browning a trial, have perhaps begun at the wrong end, and never gone on. Ask the man in' the street if he likes Browning, and in nine cases out of ten he will answer that he has not the brains to understand him. Now he has the brains, but he has not the time ; or else he has not wished to spend the necessary time, having no taste for solving puzzles. Mr. Swinburne, it is true, is supposed to have put to silence for ever, with one stroke of that magician's wand of his, which has in it at the same time something of the qualities of the giant's club, all those who dare to say that Browning is obscure. His brilliant protest, however, only tends to make us willing, if necessary, to surrender the word obscure, as perhaps not the fittest to describe poetry which blinds from " excess of light " rather than " any touch of darkness," as we all very well know. And, although we may surrender it in dealing with this especial criticism, since the whole hangs upon the meaning of the word, still the world will in all probability continue to use words in their generally accepted rather than in their academic sense ; and the thing which most of us mean by obscurity remains so long as people of average intelligence can read many of Browning's poems through, and at the end have no clear idea as to what the whole is about ; although isolated sentences may have suggested isolated pictures or thoughts. And the cause, nature, and degree of this obscurity has nothing to say to the main question ; nor has the fact that Browning's thought, when once one gets at it, is not obscure, very much to say to it ; since his thought is not his poetry. For this one reason, if for no other, Browning never has been, and never will be, a popular poet. Leaving out of consideration all those who will not read poetry at all, we have again a large number who will read poetry, but not Browning's ; finally, narrowing down the circle of his true public to include only those who

read and read again and love, we find that
it is undeniably—the few. That this may
rob him of a place among the greatest poets
of the world, his most ardent admirer will
willingly concede ; if the ardour of his admiration has not blunted his sense of proportion,
and blinded him to the value of the two-fold
test by which all artists ought to be measured,
—that of universality and of abidingness ; but
it will not rob him of his place among the
poets and the great poets, nor does it in any
way detract from his value to the individual
who has come to value him.

The esteem in which Browning has been
held has passed through many phases. First
there was wide-spread neglect. A few read
his poetry, and of that few still fewer praised.
Nor did this soon pass away. In a letter of
Mrs. Browning's, written probably in the year
1860, we find the following :—" Nobody there
(in England), except a small knot of pre-
Raffaelite men, pretend to do him justice.
Mr. Forster has done his best—in the press.
As a sort of lion, Robert has his range in
society, and, for the rest, you should see
Chapman's returns !" It was in this year 1860,

—a time when his powers were at their height, after he had produced *Men and Women* and *Paracelsus* and *Waring* and *The Pied Piper* and *The Flight of the Duchess* and *Pippa Passes* and *Christmas Eve and Easter Day*,— that in six months,—so we read,—his publishers did not dispose of one copy of his works. This he tells himself, not bitterly, rather with a kind of bluff simplicity, equally removed from hurt feeling and from affected carelessness. He did care; but he accepted the neglect with a kind of wonder just tinged with pity for the public, neither of which he thinks of concealing. For he knows that his poetry, taking it all in all, is worth reading; and yet he has learned by experience that the majority of Englishmen will not read it. These two facts he recognises, but does not try to reconcile; and he goes on writing all the same. "As I began, so I shall end," he writes, "—taking my own course, pleasing myself, or aiming at doing so; and thereby, I hope, pleasing God." People may read or not read; he has something to say, and he will say it.

Next we have the homage of an extended circle of those thinking people who have time

and patience ; but even then some courage
was necessary to profess oneself a reader of
Browning, so certain was the question to follow,
—"And you think you understand him?" a
question the answering of which taxes one, in
whatever light it may be regarded. As if one
understands the blue of the sky, or the Sistine
Madonna, or an Alpine peak, or the love of
one's friends, or a countless number of the
beautiful things with which life is crammed.

Next the appreciation of the faithful, laborious few permeated the soil around, and
Browning became very generally read by
true lovers of poetry. This was partly occa-
sioned by the difficulty becoming less. For
Browning preceded his age ; and although
he could not put himself back into the
age in which he wrote, yet in time the
age was bound to grow to him. This is
what is still happening ; for although truth
is one and eternal and universal, there is such
a thing as a Zeitgeist ; and Browning undeniably interprets the Zeitgeist of this rather
than his own age. For that which he writes
about is now in the air. It greets us from
the ephemeral literature of the day ; an appeal

to the philosophy or the view of life of Browning strikes an answering chord in the being of most people who think at all, even those who will not be induced to read his poetry for themselves; they enter upon his thought, even though they may be repelled by his presentment of it.

But this does not mean popularity. It is true that for some time he has seemed to have a certain degree of popularity; because once it became generally acknowledged among the thinkers of the day that he had a message for the world, and that he was a poet, the same was bound to become an article of the literary creed of the many who like sheep follow a lead. Then most people under a certain age who read at all, professed themselves to be "very fond of Browning." The popularity of a few of his shorter poems went up by leaps and bounds; as, for instance, *Rabbi Ben Ezra* and *Abt Vogler*. They were quoted in sermons; people who wrote letters to the newspapers talked of "all that the world's coarse thumb and finger failed to plumb," when they were accused of not doing what they ought to have done; and in the heart of the true

Browning lover consternation and woe! And then that immortal bird, that "wings and sings." Whether it is that the rhyme is catching, or in obedience to some occult law that rules the fluctuations of popular taste, that bird has seen much service. Much as one likes him, one almost wishes that he could be laid aside for a time to enjoy a well-earned rest; and one day years hence we might hear him again take up his merry pipe, and tell the world once more that life is good.

But all this was fated to pass away, and it is, in fact, in process of passing away. The latest development of popular opinion is that of the young Oxford undergraduate, who "thinks that the Browning craze is passing over; he, for his part, infinitely prefers Wordsworth." This only means that those who read Browning because other people did, are ceasing to do so; while those who read from a natural predilection continue to read; and I believe it to be true, in spite of the testimony of the keepers of public libraries that the demand for Browning's works to-day is not so great as it was five years ago, that the circle of those who read and love is on the increase.

Throughout all this Browning has suffered perhaps more than any other poet from undiscriminating blame and from undiscriminating praise. There is a large amount of off-hand condemnation of his poetry by those who have not expended the necessary time and patience on the intelligent grasping of one poem ; and who, either from hearsay, or from having actually made an attempt to read, (perhaps they have begun upon *The Red Cotton Nightcap Country*, and given the first few pages one reading), pronounce his poetry incomprehensible.

For Browning has many defects on the surface which at first sight repel the reader. Chief among them, he is undeniably obscure, as most of us understand the word. It must be said, in justice, that those who ask with a scoff, " And you understand him ? " very often scoff in sincerity ; for, no matter what our very clever friends say, the reading is not always easy.

This difficulty is, however, very much aggravated from two causes. One is the rooted idea that many people have, that Browning is obscure of malice prepense, and that he deliberately tries to puzzle us, with the result that they read his poetry with a feeling of irritation not conducive to that good understanding and generous feeling of mutual confidence with which author and reader ought to meet. Browning himself has expressly denied that he tried to puzzle people, and many indications seem to point against it. His comment on the title, "Bells and Pomegranates," which he gave to a whole series of his poems, is significant. First explaining it, he adds naïvely, and evidently in all good faith, "I supposed that the bare words in such juxtaposition would convey the desired meaning"! in spite of the fact that there is never a bell and never a pomegranate mentioned otherwise than incidentally from beginning to end! One wonders how many other obscure figures and far-fetched allusions of his may have seemed to himself equally self-luminous. Again, in describing his wife's method—one smiles at the comparison, but the words illustrate the point—he writes the following : "You are quite wrong—quite wrong" (this is in answer to a friend who has remarked that she admired his poetry more than his wife's); "She has genius ; I am only a painstaking fellow. Can't you imagine a clever sort of angel, who plots and plans, and tries to build up something — he wants to make you see it as he sees it, shows you one point of view, carries you off to another, hammering into your head the thing that he wants you to understand ; and whilst all this bother is going on, God Almighty turns you off a little star—that's the difference between us." There is abundant evidence in his poetry of this laborious and clumsy hammering out of a thought which points to the conclusion that in this matter he at least did his best ; that his obscurity is not the obscurity of Rossetti, who sometimes, in dealing with transcendental or mystical themes, designedly expresses himself vaguely, because his thought is not clear-cut, and he does not wish that it should be ; not the obscurity of William Morris who deliberately obscures the narrative of a simple incident when no purpose seems to be served by it; but rather the obscurity of one who wishes to make himself plain, but is confronted by two difficulties—the depth of his thought and his want of skill in expressing himself.

Again, there is the order in which Browning's poetry is often read. So many people

begin at the wrong end, and there are so
many wrong ends to begin at. It used to
be a custom among Browning prophets to
advise the younger disciples, or those who
aspired to discipleship, to begin with *Rabbi
Ben Ezra*, because it was easiest, and at the
same time a kind of test-piece by which it
could be decided whether they were likely ever
to become readers or not. That it is easiest
is very questionable. If one is to study a
whole scheme of philosophy, better study it
from a big book than from a little one. It is
true that the most salient points in Browning's philosophy, which elsewhere are only
hinted at, or taken for granted, are made the
main theme in *Rabbi Ben Ezra* and deliberately enunciated; but when one considers the
wide extent of the subject, and then the length
of the poem, one's brain almost reels. For
he sings of God and of the soul, of immor-
tality, of the relationship between this life
and the next, of the value of the flesh, of
the significance of pleasure, pain, difficulties,
hindrances, and failure, all in one short poem
of thirty-two stanzas! And a short summary
of a great subject is always difficult,—difficult

and delusive. One so often seems to have grasped all, when only a part has been grasped. There are, it is true, various short handbooks on such subjects as Psychology, Metaphysics, and the like, which profess to go to the root of the matter; and so they do, leaving the unwary student happily browsing upon the topmost branches, and lo! he knows it not. It is always easy to seem to understand what one does not go very deeply into. The greatest hindrance which besets any searcher after realities is not so much the incapacity to see that which is within his horizon, as the lack of that subtler instinct which tells him that there are vast tracts outside of it. "I see all," so often means,—"All that I see is all."

It is much better to have no system at all in reading Browning, but to read just what attracts among the short lyrics in any volume of selections. Of these there are always some which are reasonably intelligible on the first reading, quite plain on the second. Certainly most people can read with pleasure *May and Death, Home Thoughts from Abroad, A Lost Mistress,* or *The Last Ride Together,* long

before *Rabbi Ben Ezra.* These are taken,
not that they are of the same class, but
because the subject matter of all is within
the grasp of any ordinary intelligence, and
because two of them present slight difficulties
in the technique, which are characteristic of
Browning's style, and which, although not the
chief cause of the obscurity of Browning, are
nevertheless that cause which besets one on
first accosting him, that which stands in the
way, and effectually bars all further progress
until it is overcome. There are many people
of average intelligence, unversed in Browning's
style—not clever people—who will find that
the following two stanzas in *A Lost Mistress*
call for a second reading :—

> "For each glance of that eye so bright and black,
>   Though I keep with heart's endeavour,—
> Your voice, when you wish the snowdrops back,
>   Though it stay in my soul for ever !—
>
> Yet I will but say what mere friends say,
>   Or only a thought stronger ;
> I will hold your hand but as long as all may,
>   Or so very little longer !"

Here the thought is simplicity itself; only the
grammar of the sentence, when the stanzas are
not detached in this way, is not evident at first

sight. It is well to get over some of this before attacking Browning's philosophy. The same kind of construction occurs in *Rabbi Ben Ezra* in the following passage :—

> "Not that, amassing flowers,
> Youth sighed 'Which rose make ours,
> Which lily leave and then at best recall?'
> Not that, admiring stars,
> It yearned 'Nor Jove, nor Mars;
> Mine be some figured flame which blends,
>   transcends them all!'
>
> Not for such hopes and fears
> Annulling youth's brief years,
> Do I remonstrate :— "

but here both technique and thought tax one; a reason for reading the other first. This style of composition is not good,—let this be granted; but it is certain that it is a style that one can read oneself into and master; so that a reader of Browning can always arrive at this point, that however much the thought may tax him, the language is almost always comprehensible.

What remains always a stumbling-block,— repels those who do not know Browning, and is pain and grief to those who do and love him, is the roughness of his form, his unmusical lines, his grotesque rhymes, and the evident labour

with which his verse is built up. His flouting of
the canons of good taste has been stigmatised
even as an "impertinence." A conscious impertinence it assuredly was not. That he was careless
and slovenly is belied by the fact that he spared
no time and labour in equipping himself in
every way possible for his work. If he chooses
an historical subject, he comes to it unarmed at
no point for which reading and research can
arm him. It is the same with his science. Dr.
Berdoe has paid a high tribute to his knowledge
of the scientific subjects he deals with :—" He
(Browning) is always right," he writes. "Sometimes he appears incomprehensible. One ran-
sacks dictionaries and encyclopædias. It is they
that are defective, not Browning wanting." By
all this he sought to do honour to his poetic gift.
But while he could fittingly equip himself at all
points requiring labour and research, there were
difficulties in technique, which seem to have
been for him insurmountable.

True there are many passages in his poetry
which one cannot but feel to have been
verbally inspired ; and here there is no question of technique ; it drops out. Take the
following :—

"Therefore to whom turn I but to Thee, the ineffable Name?
  Builder and maker, Thou, of houses not made with hands!
What! have fear of change from Thee who art ever the same?
  Doubt that Thy power can fill the heart that Thy power
    expands?"

Or again,—

"A foolish thought, and worse, perhaps!
  There must be many a pair of friends
Who, arm in arm, deserve the warm
  Moon-births and the long evening-ends."

Or again, in a passage widely different, where he speaks of that third, last, best part of man, which

"tending up,
Holds, is upheld by, God, and ends the man
Upward in that dread point of intercourse,
Nor needs a place, for it returns to Him."

Here, as in countless other passages, we would not have a word different; we feel that the words come of themselves, that they cannot but come, and cannot come otherwise.

But for the most part Browning's verse, even when free from worse blemishes, lacks that note of "inevitableness" which Wordsworth finds wanting in Goethe's poetry; the steps by which the construction is built up are too evident; the work throughout bears the marks

C

of the workman's tools. He very often seems
to search laboriously for language that is
"fit and fair and simple and sufficient," as he
himself admirably expresses it, and the effort
is writ large over the whole. And some of
his greatest and noblest thoughts are expressed
in language which fails in all four points. In
Christmas Eve, for instance, there are passages
which approach very near to the sublime, but
which stop short of it, because suddenly one
feels a great jolt in the metre, or a grotesque
rhyme comes in which only provokes a smile,
where a smile is out of place. All this brings
us down into a region where we are compelled
to think of the technique, and the finer
essence of poetry evaporates; you look up, and
it is gone. But that he deliberately sets aside
the canons of taste is at least "not proven";
and it seems reasonable to believe that a
writer who shows himself laborious on the one
hand would hardly be careless and slovenly on
the other. He seems to have done everything
possible to arm himself with a sufficient
vocabulary; the man who, on deciding to
embark on the career of literature, could read
the dictionary through, was capable of

anything. This one act is significant. Rossetti,
we are told, used to read mediæval romances
in search of "stunning" words for his poetry ;
and among his unpublished works a list of
such words has been found. Rossetti, with his
matchless technique, could well afford to turn
his attention to superfluous adornments ;
Browning, aiming at nothing but expressing
himself, tries to acquire a knowledge of his
mother tongue, pure and simple. And yet it
is in some of those points upon which he has
expended most labour, that he fails.

And then there is that crying sin against
style, not so easily defined, but which all
readers of Browning know and feel, the introduction of language which belongs by right to
the sphere of logical argument into passages
where otherwise the language is that of pure
poetry. And we feel that this is deliberately
done ; for so close is the connection between
beauty of thought and beauty of form, that
they never would have come of themselves
into so alien a country. It seems as if
Browning either lacked that fine instinctive
feeling for form which preserves many a
worse poet from such incongruities, or that,

in his anxiety to express himself, he despair-
ingly resorts to any means rather than leave
the thing unsaid.   One can imagine him, in
the last extremity of the hammering process
he himself describes, saying at last, " I do not
care how I say this, if only I can succeed in
saying it at all."

The Browning lover admits all this, while
he feels at the same time that Browning
suffers at the hands of those who do not like
him from an exaggeration of these things,
and of the importance of them ; so that
either they never go on to get at the heart
of him, or, in continuing to read, they read
with a critical faculty rendered abnormally
wakeful by these frequent demands upon it ;
and we all know that this is not the condition in which we are most open to the higher
influences of art.   They are tempted to forget
what is the main office of the poet.

But Browning suffers also at the hands of
his friends.   A wicked fairy seems to have
come to his christening, and decreed that he
should never receive either praise or blame by
measure.   People generally either exalt him
beyond all others, or they will have none of

him. The critics, of course, even the most
friendly, are for the most part temperate in
their praise; but the lay reader knows no
such bounds; and one does sometimes hear
Browning called our greatest English poet,
our deepest thinker, the greatest religious
teacher in all literature; and the great shades
of Shakespeare and Dante standing by and
saying never a word! What people mean by
these wild statements is probably this,—that
they like Browning better than any other
poet; and that he has taught them more than
any one else has taught them; which is a
very different thing and a thing readily con-
ceivable. We are influenced as to what we like
by many circumstances, notably by mood, by
the time in which we live, and by our individual
needs and bent. The fact is, what we like has
nothing to say to it, that is, what isolated
individuals like. The universal, abiding favour
of mankind has a great deal, has everything to
say to it. And the favour in which Browning
is held is certainly not universal; whether or
not it will abide, it is idle to speculate.

That Browning has failed to catch the ear
of the mob cannot be ignored. "But he is

too deep, too subtle," it is urged ; "if he
were shallower, he would be more popular."
This sounds plausible, and is in part true,
but it is fallacious.   It is true that a
shallow poet may catch the ear of the mob,
but poets not shallow can do the same, with
this difference, that the power of the one
abides ; that of the other does not.   The
shallow poet does not permanently keep his
place in the heart of the mob.   And if
Browning does not appeal to all, it is not of
necessity because he is subtle.   Shakespeare
was more subtle.   But the man in the street
in Elizabeth's reign could enjoy Shakespeare,
and the man in the street can enjoy him to-
day.   For, no matter how deep Shakespeare
may go, he never overlooks the elementary
human emotions ; and while he gives us a
Hamlet, who defies psychological analysis,
he gives us at the same time a Gonzalo
and a Bassanio.   Side by side with Lady
Macbeth and Cleopatra, we have Hermia and
Celia.   And the man in the street who will
never read *Paracelsus* will read *Hamlet* with
pleasure ; for, although the problems which
perplex Hamlet are at least as deep and

complicated as anything that we find in
Paracelsus, yet we have at the same time the
play of the every-day emotions, love, hate,
pity, revenge, jealousy; and this is just what
makes the difference.   We all remember how
we read *Hamlet* when we were children, read it
happily, nothing doubting; and never dreamed
that there was more in it than what we saw.
The condition of Hamlet's mind troubled us
not at all; we did not know that there was any
difficulty here; but we knew that his father
was dead, and that he was very unhappy, and
that he had a bad mother and a wicked uncle
and a faithful friend and a true lover; further,
we knew that a ghost wandered in and out of
the scene in a delightfully promiscuous fashion;
and how entrancingly. interesting it all was!
Shakespeare gives us all life; the superficial
truth of things, and the deep underlying truth of
things; so that the shallow and the superficial
can come and find themselves mirrored there;
and those who "live from a great depth of
being" can come and find themselves likewise.
The philosophy of Shakespeare may pass over
the heads of the many; but his presentation of
the story does not, and the power of the living

personality of his men and women does not;
while the charm of his fine, careless, genial ease
of production acts like a spell upon many who
never speculate as to what it is that thus holds
them, and know nothing of the depths from
which it all springs. Browning, on the other
hand, gives us very often only the subtle and
metaphysical; and for those who cannot enter
into this, there is then nothing left. Shakespeare speaks to grave and gay, to wise and
foolish; Browning has no words, or few words,
for the foolish; thereby placing himself in a
lower rank as poet.

This he recognises himself in theory. In the
mouth of Aprile, his typical poet, he places these
words :—

> " . . . . For common life, its wants
> And ways, would I set forth in beauteous hues;
> The lowest hind should not possess a hope,
> A fear, but I'd be by him, saying better
> Than he his own heart's language. . .
> . . . . nor this
> Would need a meaner spirit than the first ;
> Nay, 'twould be but the self-same spirit, clothed
> In humbler guise; but still the self-same spirit ;
> As one spring wind unbinds the mountain snows
> And comforts violets in their hermitage."

Wordsworth himself could not have said more.
Again, when Browning wishes to give an

example of the pure spirit of poetry, which abides, its power unabated, throughout the ages, he reminds us how,—

> " . . . . . Fleet the years,
> And still the poet's page holds Helena
> At gaze from topmost Troy—'But where are they,
> My brothers, in the armament I name,
> Hero by hero? Can it be that shame
> For their lost sister holds them from the war?'—
> Knowing not they already slept afar,
> Each of them in his own dear native land."

Thus true and wide-reaching was Browning's theory of poetry. But the bent of his mind led him to feel interested rather in the complicated and the unusual than in the simple and the every-day; and consequently by far the largest part of his poetry deals with this. The one all-absorbing subject of interest to him was the development of a soul;—"Little else is worth study," he writes; and although we are all actors in this drama, the study of our parts does not interest us all. For this one reason alone Browning will never appeal to all.

In all this there is no question of popularity in the generally accepted sense of the word. There is a vicious use of the word universality, by which it is taken to mean that which

appeals to a mob of the commonplace, with
the higher element of the human race left
out; whereas, in its true significance, it
means that which appeals to all, high as
well as low, but especially the former. An
appeal of this kind is the triumph of our
very greatest in art. But coming next in
rank are those who appeal to the finer spirit
of the race only. They do not possess this
quality of universality, but neither do those
who appeal to the mob only. Neither can
stand this test ; but the former are true
artists, the latter are not.

By some, who take an extreme view of the
value of this quality of universality, that which
fails to appeal to all is placed outside the domain of true art. Tolstoi finds it intolerable
that a workman of average intelligence cannot
understand an opera of Wagner's, if Wagner is
to hold rank as a true musician. Tolstoi, of
course, does not hold any opinion with a slack
grasp; but one very often hears from others
as well opinions which are a modification of
this. This is not, however, the judgment of
all deep thinkers. Wordsworth, in the essay
which once formed the preface to the first

edition of the *Lyrical Ballads*, dealing with
this subject, emphatically rejects popularity
as any test of a poet's work. Poetry of the
best kind, he insists, must be satisfied for a
season with few and scattered readers, "since
there never was a period in which vicious
poetry, of some kind or other, has not
excited more zealous admiration, and been
far more generally read than good." Does
he then belittle and despise the judgment of
the people? No. For all good poetry sur-
vives. "And how doth it survive but through
the people? What preserves it but their
intellect and wisdom?" But it must be the
intellect and wisdom of one age continually
corrected by that of the next. The guardians
of the life of a true work of art are indeed
the people, but not the people at its lowest,
in a transient mood, rather that spirit of the
people that abides, which ratifies in this age
the decisions of the last, that great spirit
of humanity, which is not of to-day, or of
yesterday, or of to-morrow, but of all three :—

> " ' . . . Past and future are the wings
> On whose support, harmoniously conjoined,
> Moves the great spirit of human knowledge.'

The voice that issues from this spirit is the
vox populi which the deity inspires." So wrote
Wordsworth, the poet of " joy in widest
commonalty spread."

It is well to bear all this in mind in face
of the everlasting reproach brought up against
Browning, and the readers of Browning, that
he is the poet of the few. He is the poet of
the few ; and therefore he does not take his
place among the greatest of all, those giants
in art whom we can count on the fingers of
one hand. But when we have said this, all has
not been said. He is not forthwith doomed
and shut out from Parnassus. He does not
appeal to all ; but neither does Milton, nor
Wordsworth, nor Wagner, nor Turner.

Let the worst be frankly conceded. He is
obscure, yes ; often faulty in form, rough
inharmonious, yes ; his appeal is limited, yes.
The Browning lover knows all about this. It
is Browning himself who tells us that, although
love is painted blind, he is of all most clear-
sighted. Who can see blemishes so well as
he who is most affected by them ; and that
is surely the lover. But the Browning lover
is " not careful to answer in this matter." All

that the detractors say may be true. He is
not in this plane; the grounds of his allegiance
are elsewhere. It is as though some one
attacked the colour of your friend's hair, or
the house that he lives in. You may argue
the point to show loyalty, and in the interests
of truth and justice; you may wish that the
matter were put fairly, if put at all; but the
direct issue concerns you not at all; you are
not in that region. What Browning is to the
individual to whom he speaks of that which lives
in the inmost soul, is apart from all these questions which are the main concern of the critic.

There is one test of a poet, not a test
of his rank, but none the less the all import-
ant one to the individual, which Browning
bears triumphantly,—can we do without him?
This question will often help to keep the
balance, when the fancy of the hour, or when
any other surface circumstance causes us to
attach a value not altogether the true one
to any work of art; or when we are in danger
of losing our sense of proportion when held
by some powerful attraction. If some of us
who love Rossetti, and who will read Rossetti
when we do not want to read Shakespeare, were

asked,—which can we the better do without,
Hamlet or *The Blessed Damozel*, if one or the
other were to be wiped out as if never written?
what would the answer be? It is given with
no uncertain voice; yes, the Blessed Damozel,
her footsteps sounding all along "the echoing
stair," would recede further and further into the
distance; and we should turn round to find the
Dane in his place. Comparisons are always
unfair and generally ungenerous, but there is
this point here, we cannot do without Browning,
that is, those of us who know his worth. What
would happen if any dreadful choice were put
before us, we cannot picture; but we are quite
sure about this, we cannot let Browning go.

For Browning's supreme title of honour is
that he is in the lives of many something
distinctive and unique. Many people, looking
back, can say that he has spoken to them
as no one else has spoken; and that life and
death and all things wear a different aspect
for his handling. This is saying much; but
many will bear me out that these are the words
of truth and sobriety.

Exception may, it is true, be taken, and has
been taken, to any such estimate under two

heads; one, that what he says has been said before; the other, that it is not what he says which is the main work of the poet; that to value Browning for this reason is to value him as a philosopher and a teacher, but not as a poet. The answer to the first objection answers the second also. The bald prose of much that he says has been said before. It is true that others before Browning have said,—there is a God ;—man has an immortal soul ;—there is an after-life ;—this life is a probation ;—this life is good. But Browning gives us the Seer's interpretation of these things, that is, he endeavours to give us that truest truth of them which so often eludes thought as well as language, the " breath and finer spirit " of them, if one may so apply Wordsworth's phrase. And what, after all, is the prime thing needful in a poet ? Surely it is to have something to communicate which cannot be expressed except by art. If we were asked what are the three chief requirements of a poet, we should be inclined to answer,—" First, insight ; secondly, insight ; thirdly, insight "; did we not know that " mute inglorious Miltons " undeniably exist. We are rudely recalled to a due

the relative importance of matter and form in poetry. "The prime concern of the artist must be with his vehicle of expression," one asserts baldly. "But you must first have something to express," another urges. "True," the first returns, "but if your main concern is to express your thought, why not use the ordinary language of prose?" What does it all amount to? Is the real contention a matter of words or things? In truth, when one ranges from Aristotle's celebrated dictum,—"Poetry must possess a higher truth and a higher seriousness than prose," to Coleridge's definition,—"Poetry is that species of composition which is opposed to works of science by proposing for its *immediate* object pleasure not truth ;" from Schopenhauer,—"All is a question of style now with poetry," to Ruskin,—"No weight nor mass nor beauty of execution can outweigh one grain or fragment of thought," in this Babel of tongues it is well to possess one's soul in patience, and to withdraw oneself awhile from the region of criticism, where the very air is darkened by a crowd of "words—words—words,"—strange winged creatures which change their form and colouring for every different combination in

D

which they are found, for every different point
of view from which they are regarded, and
ask oneself what one really thinks and feels;
what part does poetry bear in one's own life.
Perhaps Matthew Arnold's sober and balanced
words come nearest to expressing that reality:
—" Poetry is the most perfect speech of man,—
that in which he comes nearest to being able
to utter the truth ;" for here he does not forget
or ignore that the vehicle affects the utterance
of the truth, while at the same time the
utterance of the truth is the main concern of
the poet, that for which the vehicle exists.

Those who insist that style is everything in
poetry seem to be ignoring this—that there
is an essential difference between poetry and
prose, not alone in the manner in which the
thing is said, but in the nature of the thing
said. The prose writer records, narrates, argues,
exhorts; the poet, first seeing that which all
men do not see, endeavours to show this to
the world; the one is the work of the intellect,
the other that of the soul. It is true that,
even for the poet, the intellect is pressed to
the service, but the work is not primarily
intellectual work. This broad distinction exists

before we touch the question of form. If a verse-writer only says that which can be said equally well in prose, however good his form may be, he is no poet.

A confusion arises through not recognising this first principle in the world of art—that there is much which one sees with the inner eye of the soul absolutely incommunicable through the ordinary language of prose, incommunicable through any medium except art, and even by art only imperfectly communicable. This must be borne in mind when we are confronted with this statement: the thought in a poem is not the poetry. Of course it is not. A thought can be expressed in prose. But when some critics say, " Browning's 'message,' so-called, must be discounted in any consideration of his rank as a poet," it is well to ask this question first: "What is the nature of the message?" If a message only means a communication addressed to the intellect, and appreciable only by the intellect, then the delivery of a message is distinctly outside the sphere of poetry. All are practically agreed as to this. But if a message can mean, as many of us use the word, something more — a subtle something

which eludes thought, and the expression of
which eludes the ordinary language of every-
day intercourse, something which is appreciable only by a subtler faculty than the
intellect, then all art is in the truest sense
a message. And when Browning, first seeing that which all men do not see, shows
us this, then he is in the truest sense a
poet.   This act of interpretation may be
done well or ill ; the question of prime importance is,—is it done?   Take some of those
poems of Browning's in which all his worst
defects congregate, and whatever their exact
rank as poetry may be, they find their place
in no other sphere of human activity ; this
is their natural home and their own place.
To say that we have known all before, because all has been said before, is to say that,
because we have read the old yellow book
which contains the crude facts of the Frances-
chini murder case, we know all that *The
Ring and the Book* says.   To present such
philosophy of life as Browning's is in any
form constructed on the scientific method,
and displaying as well as calling for mere
hard thinking, would be to present it with

the finer essence, the *vraie vérité* of it left
out. For the presentation of just this the
artistic medium was absolutely necessary to
Browning ; but to follow this up by saying :
" Discount Browning's thought, discount his
message ;   it has all been said before," this
is truly to read Browning with Browning left
out ; it is, as he himself would express it,
" to take the film that's furled about a star
for the star's self."

These two points the Browning lover is
insistent upon ;—the value of Browning to
him lies in that which he says, not in his
manner of saying it ; and Browning speaks
to him as a poet, not primarily as a thinker.
To yield these would be to belie his own
experience.

And the Browning lover goes further and
asks,—has any one, indeed, in literature, among
all those who, he is told, have said it all
before, combined just such a profound and
dominating realisation of a future life with
the same keen sense of the value and significance of this ; painted with so strong and
yet so tender a hand the figure of that
love which holds both in the hollow of

her hand ; apprehended with just such a
true and penetrating insight the meaning
of all that baffles and hinders us here, nay, the
meaning of evil itself, the need and the transi-
toriness of it ; so pierced through the crust of
outward conditions as to find the pure gold
under the most unpromising exterior, in the
most unexpected places? Note the marvellous
touches, prodigally scattered throughout his
poetry, by which he shows that, though the stars
in their courses may seem to fight for the
triumph of evil, yet that it is good that
triumphs. Such is the spark struck from out
the soul of the "polished snob" in *The Inn
Album*, — a bright gleam of light which
suddenly flashes before our eyes in the midst
of a dreary waste of sin and falsehood :—

> " But this — this only— . . .
> I believe somehow in your purity
> Perfect as ever."

One such touch as this is to some of us worth
many pages of the "felicitous" utterance of a
Keats, beautiful and true as such an utterance is.
The poets who show to us the soul that dwells in
all beauty, perform for us no mean service ; for
truth is truth ; there is no greater or less ; "all

service ranks the same" here as elsewhere.   But
more powerfully operative upon the daily lives
of us, who live in the midst of this mystery of
evil, are the words of one who shows to us the
" soul of good in things evil," of " one who
.   .   .   . never dreamed, though right were
worsted, wrong would triumph."   In all this we
cannot place the poetry of Browning in a region
apart from the strong and luminous personality
which is behind it all.   The man who, at the age
of twenty, wrote, " I believe in God and truth
and love," and who, clinging to this faith
unwavering for the following fifty-seven years of
his life, died with the same on his lips, is a
personality that must not be discounted in
any estimate of his poetry ; for, after all,
this was the rock whence it was hewn.

It is all these things in combination which
give to Browning his unique power.   It
is not a question of rank, or of assigning to
him his proper place when measured with
others ; if indeed this can ever be assigned to
any poet, seeing how infinite are the varieties
of gifts.   As we cannot compare one flower
with another, nor the sea with the sky, neither
can we compare one aspect of the truth with

another, and place one first, another last. And
to Browning we assign no rank when we say
that he has a power that is all his own. While
above the gates of death he has erected a
triumphal arch, inscribed with the legend,—
" This is the threshold of boundless life," he
shows us how, all the time, above this earth
too, with all its dark places, is stretched the
infinite expanse of the blue of God's own
heaven.

PARACELSUS.

I.

PARACELSUS ASPIRES.

"Where'er you gazed, there stood a star!"

"I HAVE endeavoured to write a poem, not a drama," Browning writes in his preface to the earliest edition of *Paracelsus*; anticipating the adverse criticism with which his work might be met, if "judged by principles upon which it was never moulded, and subjected to a standard to which it was never meant to conform." The event has proved that one part of the apology was not necessary. Among the many sins laid to the charge of Browning by the critics of *Paracelsus*, his designed neglect of the laws of the drama has not often been brought forward. But with the words "I have endeavoured to write a poem," he claims for himself—incidentally, it is true—

that which has very often been ignored by his
readers.   There are, in fact, many points of
interest in *Paracelsus* which lie outside the
domain of poetry ; as in a picture many arts
of the mere draughtsman may arrest the eye,
and challenge criticism.   There is the question
of the historical Paracelsus, of the science of
the day, of the philosophy of Paracelsus, and
of Browning's own philosophy ; and all this has
a tendency to make us forget that the whole
is primarily a product not of the mind, but of
the soul ; that it is not an act of reason, but
an act of sight ; in a word, that it is a poem ;
and as such appeals to a subtler sense than
historian, scientist, or philosopher can touch.

Throughout we see the subordinating
of all else to this one aim of giving a
poetical, that is, a true and deep - reaching
interpretation of the subject.   Take one instance of this from Browning's treatment of
history.   He comes to the task of writing
Paracelsus steeped in the history of the time.
This he considers the necessary preparation.
But he knows that his art is something above
and beyond all this.   When he finds that he
can better show the inner truth of the man

Paracelsus through the agency of an incident deliberately created for the purpose than in many passages of his life for which he has the warrant of history, he unhesitatingly and without apology creates the character of Aprile and the scene with Aprile. This is an example of his method throughout.

Paracelsus is the story of the life of a soul,—that mysterious thing whose motions may be swayed by reason, but which take their rise elsewhere; which manifests itself in action, but which no action fully reveals; that inner truth of a man, not that which knows, much less that which does, but that which *is*. It deals with no less a subject than life itself, and further and more particularly with the especial problems which life holds for the chosen few who are especially dowered above their fellows. For it is to those who are thus set on high that the mystery of life is deepest. The commonplace man lives all his life among supernatural things, and does not know it. The veil that hides them is impenetrable. If one day it were by chance drawn aside, he could exclaim with Jacob,—" Surely the Lord was in this place, and I knew it not . . . .

How dreadful is this place!" The sky, the
sea, mountain and lake, all the marvels of the
physical universe, may be to him objects of
beauty, but they are not objects of wonder;
they are to him what that immortal primrose
was to Peter Bell, nothing more. Not that
the blindest has not his moments of insight;—

> " So glorious is our nature, so august
> Man's inborn, uninstructed impulses,
> His naked spirit so majestical ; "

but what come to one man in "flashes struck
from midnights," in the form of dim surmisings
which he is only partly conscious of, and in no
wise understands, at best fleeting, leaving but
little trace upon the being, are to another
abiding realities. Such a man, living and
moving among common things, knows that
he is among supernatural things always; and
all life is one great mystery—a mystery
not of necessity impenetrable, for the pure
in heart hold the key; but nevertheless a
mystery, at once stimulating, repelling, awe-
inspiring. And the main problem is surely
this—how harmonise life? how reconcile our
brightest visions, that which we feel in every
motion of our being to be the only true and

the eternal, with all the hindrances and limitations which beset us in our every-day existence
here in this work-a-day world? It is not
altogether the old antagonism, between flesh
and spirit, although this does enter in; nor
yet that view of life as a whole which finds
an inherent antagonism between this life and
the next; for, even for those who most
fully recognise that if man is endowed with
a body as well as a soul, God gave both, and
"gifts should prove their use;" even for those
who most emphatically disclaim any contempt
for this life, any looking upon it as "a make-
shift, a mere foil, how fair so ever, to some
fine life to come," the question comes up again
and again—how harmonise life? How can one
reconcile the insufficiency of life here even at
its best, our half lights, ineffectual strivings,
constant failures to realise in its perfection
even the smallest good, with life's possibilities,
and the high destiny of man, body and soul?

To Paracelsus at nineteen the problem was
insoluble; it was not, he judged, meant to
be solved. It was vain to attempt to reconcile
things inherently antagonistic. With the sharp
logic, the headlong consistency of extreme youth,

he hurls back a contemptuous "No" to the
friend who bids him take life as he finds it, with
its joys and sorrows, hopes and fears, insuffici-
encies and failures, and live it, a man among his
fellow men, while all the time harbouring within
him the consciousness of a high vocation.

Many causes combined at this time to make
him speak this emphatic "No." For Paracelsus
was one pre-eminently set on high. The burden
of genius was laid upon him. He saw where
other men were blind, or at best dimly dis-
cerned :—

> " I stood at first where all aspire at last
> To stand : the secret of the world was mine.
> I knew, I felt (perception unexpressed,
> Uncomprehended by our narrow thought,
> But somehow felt and known in every shift
> And change in the spirit,—nay, in every pore
> Of the body, even,)—what God is, what we are,
> What life is."

Further, he believed that he was thus exceptionally dowered, because an exceptional task
awaited him in the world ; and that some power,
not himself, called him out—out :

> " ——I, singled out for this, the One !
> Think, think ! the wide East, where all wisdom sprung ;
> The bright South, where she dwelt ; the hopeful North
> All are passed o'er—it lights on me ! "

And he was only nineteen years old. To him no compromise seemed possible; to the call he must either make the ready answer or else "the great refusal." No such thing as the adjusting of his ideals to the requirements of circumstances occurred to him. To him the lowering of an ideal once conceived was the betrayal of a trust. Neither did any small prize by the way allure him; there was to be no patient heaping up of gain upon gain; he desired rather

"——to gain one prize
In place of many—the secret of the world,
Of man, and man's true purpose, path, and fate."

With this aim, vast and shadowy in the distance, he turned his eyes persistently away from all that lay in his path. He looked for no help from the work of other men; for had not all hitherto failed? The past was barren, the present dull, easily satisfied with small successes, which in the light of the absolute were unsuccess. The joys of every-day flesh and blood existence were hindrances. Men, with their petty knowledge, their still more petty loves and hates, he despised. It is true that he loved his friends; Festus, the elder-brother friend, loyal and devoted; Michal,

with the heart of a child, she, who would " sing
alone, birdlike," her face ever wearing

> "————that quiet and peculiar light
> Like the dim circlet floating round a pearl."

But their love, though sweet, was rather the
tender accompaniment to his real life outside
of them than any essential part of it. For
love, and all the emotional side of life, was what
he judged he must turn his back upon; and
although all that he sought was for the benefit
of mankind at large, yet he despised his fellow
men:

> "————I seemed to long
> At once to trample on, yet save mankind,
> To make some unexampled sacrifice
> On their behalf, to wring some wondrous good
> From heaven or earth for them, to perish, winning
> Eternal weal in the act: as who should dare
> Pluck out the angry thunder from its cloud,
> That, all its gathered flame discharged on him,
> No storm might threaten summer's azure sleep:
> Yet never to be mixed with men so much
> As to have part even in my own work, share
> In my own largess. Once the feat achieved,
> I would withdraw from their officious praise,
> Would gently put aside their profuse thanks.
> Like some knight traversing a wilderness,
> Who, on his way, may chance to free a tribe
> Of desert-people from their dragon-foe;
> When all the swarthy race press round to kiss

His feet, and choose him for their king, and yield
Their poor tents, pitched among the sand-hills, for
His realm : and he points, smiling, to his scarf
Heavy with riveled gold, his burgonet
Gay set with twinkling stones—and to the East,
Where these must be displayed !''

This, which he characterised to Festus as his
" first mad impulse," when, after the calm and
seclusion of his childhood's home, he " first
viewed the thronged, the everlasting concourse
of mankind," was the attitude towards his fellow
men to which he constantly returned at this
time.

It had not always been so with him. In his
early boyhood, the love of his friends, Einsiedeln
and its green hills, had been all the world to him.
It is true that, in the light of after-years, looking
back, he knew that from a child he had been
" possessed by a true fire ; " but he did not at
first understand it, or think of giving it vent :

"I was not born
Informed and fearless from the first, but shrank
From all that marked me out apart from men :
I would have lived their life, and died their death,
Lost in their ranks, eluding destiny."

But destiny chose for its instrument Festus,—
patient, plodding Festus. He it was who, first
E

noting some unusual power in the dreamy boy, urged him to know mankind, and to know himself, to discover man's end and God's will, and to endeavour to realise them in his life. But Festus, limited and practical, little guessed what the end would be when, hoping only for Paracelsus a high place among his fellows, nothing more, he induced him to enter the school of the then famous Trithemius at Würzburg. Here Paracelsus began his studies,

> " In that dim chamber where the noonstreaks peer
> Half frightened by the awful tomes around."

At first, Festus reminds him,

> "————not one youth
> Of those so favoured, whom you now despise,
> Came earnest as you came, resolved, like you,
> To grasp all and retain all, and deserve
> By patient toil a wide renown like his."

But Festus soon found that the spirit to which he had thus helped to reveal its own powers, took a flight far beyond anything that he had calculated upon. He had been ambitious for Paracelsus, but it was with a reasoned and temperate ambition. The well-worn highway in the broad light of the sun had seemed to him to be the fitting scene of his successes.

He shrank from the unknown, the unprecé-
dented, and had never dreamed of his entering
upon a course that would shut him out from
the common life of men. But who can set
to the spirit of man a bound that it may not
pass; or what man can rule the spirit of his
brother? The struggle of Festus to stay the
flight of Paracelsus was vain

> " as though a mother hoped
> To stay the lusty manhood of the child
> Once weak upon her knees;"

and soon we find him gazing with wide-open
eyes of astonishment at that which his modest
efforts have called forth. So must Aladdin
have gazed at the bright spirit which appeared
when first he rubbed his lamp. But Paracelsus decries this amazement as an incon-
sistency, for his present attitude is, he urges,
but the logical outcome of the beginning to
which Festus pointed him. Festus has been
with him up to a certain point, the point of
action, and here he holds back. They have
agreed as to their "best scheme of life;"
agreed further, that "faith should be acted
upon." Finally, Paracelsus goes on to pro-

pose a definite plan of action, but here Festus
stops short—

> "————so that at last
> It all amounts to this—the sovereign proof
> That we devote ourselves to God, is seen
> In living just as though no God there were;
> A life which, prompted by the sad and blind
> Folly of man, Festus abhors the most;
> But which these tenets sanctify at once,
> Though to less subtle wits it seems the same,
> Consider it how they may."

Thus does the cruel, uncompromising logic
of youth confront the shrinking back of a
man who was quite willing to rest happily
upon the reflection—

> "What hand and brain went ever paired?
> What heart alike conceived and dared?
> What act proved all its thought had been?
> What will but felt the fleshly screen?"

With Paracelsus to conceive was to dare, to
think was to act; the fleshly screen was a
hindrance, but one that he was determined
to overcome.

And he had tried the beaten track at first.
He had begun by plunging into the pursuits
of his fellows, in the school of Tritheim, not
asking what the ultimate goal was; but amid
a throng who struggled, he struggled too.

But soon he felt growing, and gradually
taking shape within him, the conviction that
the partial knowledge which was all that the
best of his companions was aiming at, could
never satisfy him. And then followed a time
that he would willingly " slur over," during
which the iron hand of " a slow and strangling
failure" was upon him :—

> " We aspired alike,
> Yet not the meanest plodder Tritheim counts
> A marvel, but was all-sufficient, strong,
> Or staggered only at his own vast wits ;
> While I was restless, nothing satisfied,
> Distrustful, most perplexed."

He did so much less than the others ; he loathed
himself as weak compared with them ; " yet
somehow felt a mighty power was brooding,
taking shape within him." At last there was
" a sudden pause, a total change ; " and now all
the vague, dimly understood promptings of his
boyhood gathered force, until at last, one night ;
—for Paracelsus, like many another could lay
his hand upon one day in his life, which
changed for him the whole face of the world,—
" what was a speck expands into a star," and
the blind saw. It was no new knowledge
forced in upon an alien soul ; it was rather that

a veil which had obscured the light was all at
once drawn aside, and he saw that which had
always been close to him, the life of his life.
And the hand which drew aside the veil was
from without :

> " One night
> When, as I sat revolving it and more,
> A still voice from without said—' Seest thou not,
> ' Desponding child, whence spring defeat and loss ?
> ' Even from thy strength.   Consider : hast thou gazed
> ' Presumptuously on wisdom's countenance,
> ' No veil between ; and can thy faltering hands,
> ' Unguided by the brain the sight absorbs,
> ' Pursue their task as earnest blinkers do
> ' Whom radiance ne'er distracted ?   Live their life
> ' If thou wouldst share their fortune, choose their eyes
> ' Unfed by splendour.   *Let each task present*
> ' *Its petty good to thee.*   Waste not thy gifts
> ' In profitless waiting for the gods' descent,
> ' But have some idol of thine own to dress
> ' With their array.   Know, not for knowing's sake,
> ' But to become a star to men for ever ;
> ' Know, for the gain it gets, the praise it brings,
> ' The wonder it inspires, the love it breeds :
> ' *Look one step onward, and secure that step !* ' "

And he smiled as one never smiles but once.

This is the true Browning theme, familiar to
all readers of Browning, even the most casual ;—
the burden of the message which, in season and
out of season, in its manifold aspects, he
constantly repeats ; the significance of apparent

failure ; the old contrast between the " high
man " and the " low man " of *The Grammarian's Funeral ;* the meaning of the " broken
arcs " to those to whom the vision of the
" perfect round " somewhere, afar, has been
vouchsafed. Paracelsus has seemed to fail ; but
—" what is our failure here but a triumph's evidence for the fulness of the days ? " If he would
be what men call successful, let him choose a
task well within his grasp ; let him " draw a
circle premature, heedless of far gain." But if
he proudly refuse thus to " discount life," then he
must throw himself on God,—" He loves the
burthen ; " he must disregard immediate results,
and see in his apparent failure only a proof and
a natural consequence of the extent of his aim.

It is now that he first discovers what that
aim is, and knows with a sudden lightning-
flash that it is nothing less than

> " ——*to comprehend the works of God,*
> *And God himself, and all God's intercourse*
> *With the human mind.*"

He looks the task full in the face, and knows
that the path is " hard for flesh to tread
therein, imbued with frailty ; " that it must
be undertaken for God's sake and for man's,

apart from all reward, that "in itself alone shall its reward be;" but he is all at once "endued with comprehension and a steadfast will;" and his brow is sealed to the work.

And now thenceforward "all things wore a different hue, pregnant with vast consequence, teeming with grand result, loaded with fate." That he does not see the goal distinctly is to him only the seal to his mission, the proof that this is no "arrogantly self-inflicted task," but rather his ready answer to the will of God who calls him. He is not going out in the pursuit of a goal arbitrarily chosen by himself, but in the effort to be true to the inner life of him which urges him on :—

> "——What fairer seal
> Shall I require to my authentic mission
> Than this fierce energy?—this instinct striving
> Because its nature is to strive?—enticed
> By the security of no broad course,
> Without success forever in its eyes!
> . . . . . . Be sure that God
> Ne'er dooms to waste the strength he deigns impart!
> Ask the geier-eagle why she stoops at once
> Into the vast and unexplored abyss,
> What full-grown power informs her from the first,
> Why she not marvels, strenuously beating
> The silent, boundless regions of the sky!"

And further this vital energy within him

moves in answer to a power, which is, he
repeatedly insists, without him. To the
question of Festus as to whether he discerns
the path as clearly as the purpose, or again
the purpose as clearly as his own yearning
to go out, he answers fearlessly,—not without a pause, but advisedly and fearlessly,—
" What if it be so ? " For he has not
chosen the task. He goes out because he
is called. Hence that the goal is shadowy,
matters little ; that the path is untrodden,
matters not at all ; that he should rise to
the call is for him the one matter of paramount importance :

> "————I profess no other share
> In the selection of my lot, than this
> My ready answer to the will of God
> Who summons me to be his organ. All
> Whose innate strength supports them shall succeed
> No better than the sages."   .   .   .
>
> .   .   .   .
> .   .   .   .
>
> "————I go to prove my soul !
> I see my way as birds their trackless way.
> I shall arrive ! what time, what circuit first,
> I ask not : but unless God send his hail
> Or blinding fireballs, sleet or stifling snow,
> In some time, his good time, I shall arrive :
> He guides me and the bird.   In his good time ! "

One loves to dwell on this picture of Paracelsus in his youth,—the luminous insight, the indomitable faith, the teeming, tumultuous life. Festus is silent before it ; the commonplace finds and recognises its own level in the presence of that higher thing, which, uncomprehended, is yet felt to be greater than itself. Michal, too, is silent ; but Michal, the pure in heart, believing where she cannot see or understand, and thus seeing that which is hidden from the wise, recognises truth on the instant, never mistakes the signs ; as the deep calls to the deep, and fire answers fire. To the question of Paracelsus,—" Do you believe I shall accomplish this ? " her answer falls prompt and clear,—" I ever did believe ! " The same magnetic fire seems to touch even the dullest reader who takes up this first book of *Paracelsus*. The very atmosphere is impregnated with life ; while the spirit involuntarily goes out into those trackless regions where live all unnamed and unnamable aspirations.

Upon all this the word " failure " falls like something altogether incongruous, unexpected,

impossible.   And yet, when we next see
Paracelsus, nine years later, this is the word
which comes uppermost.   When we stand
before the picture of Paracelsus in the house
of the Greek astrologer in Constantinople we
can only ask ourselves,—has he indeed
failed ? why to so fair a morning should
succeed so dark a noontide ? was it all a
mistake ? has he been wrong from the first ?
The answer to all this is emphatically,—he
was right and not wrong ; wholly right in
the main, not wholly wrong even in his
mistakes.   The whole understanding of at
least the Paracelsus of Browning depends on
duly recognising just this,—the vision of his
boyhood was true.   To look upon him as
one who throughout a confused and storm-
tossed youth followed wandering fires, but
who on his deathbed saw light at last,
involves an entire failure to grasp at least
Browning's conception of the man.   It is
true that when he brought down his vast,
stupendous aim of devoting himself to the
glory of God and the good of his fellow-
men into the region of practical human
activities, he mistook the means to the end,

true also that he failed to see what human
nature really meant, and that from the actual
fight he did not come out unspotted, that
from time to time lower ambitions and
passions made a slave of him ; but never
does he deny the heavenly vision.   A true
fire from God possessed him, a fire which
he did not always understand himself ; for
what man can sound the hidden depths of
his own spirit ? but none the less a true
fire :—

> " I knew not then
> What whispered in the evening, and spoke out
> At midnight.   If some mortal, born too soon,
> Were laid away in some great trance—the ages
> Coming and going all the while—till dawned
> His true time's advent ; and could then record
> The words they spoke who kept watch by his bed,—
> Then I might tell more of the breath so light
> Upon my eyelids, and the fingers light
> Among my hair.   Youth is confused ; yet never
> So dull was I but, when that spirit passed,
> I turned to him, scarce consciously, as turns
> A water-snake when fairies cross his sleep."

It is true that, for one horrible moment in the
house of the astrologer the despairing cry is
wrung from him,—" Ha, have I, after all,
mistaken the wild nurseling of my breast ? "
—the saddest words in the whole poem ; but

it is only for the moment; and it is significant that the doubt is immediately followed by a dread that he is going mad, and a prayer that God will spare his mind. The true Paracelsus, in his right mind, could never doubt just this; and it is a fact that at this and at no other point does this especial dread come to him. For, in truth, the last agony of despair is reserved not for those who fail themselves, but for those whose ideals fail. If, outside human blindness, weakness, or sin, still "heaven's blue above us," all is not lost; but "when God fails —despair!" And Paracelsus failing because he could not always see the light is a totally different thing from Paracelsus failing because his light was no light.

Why then did he not accomplish that which he set out to do, that which he was so confident of being able to do? Before seeing this it is necessary to have a clear idea of what his aim exactly was, not alone in its general tendency, but in its particular bent; translating it from the language of poetry into the ordinary language of every-day effort and attainment; for, if we would see how Paracelsus failed, we must first see the practical working means which he adopted to reach a definite end.

A distinct theory of the universe underlay all his speculations and researches. The divine spirit, of whom are all things, was everywhere in the world. It manifested itself in many ways, but in itself was one. Throughout all nature, inanimate as well as animate, the same spirit was at work, the same spirit was the life of all things that live: God is he

> " From whom all being emanates, all power
> Proceeds ; in whom is life for evermore,
> Yet whom existence in its lowest form
> Includes."

Thus all things are one. This is not the crude pantheism of the time of the historical Paracelsus, but a genuine nineteenth-century pantheism, subtle and metaphysical ; and it culminates in a scheme of evolution distinctly modern. For Browning, like Paracelsus, preceded his age ; and writing in 1835, at the age of twenty-three, many years before Darwin and Wallace gave to the world the theory of evolution which we associate with their names, he certainly foreshadows, if he does not anticipate some of their main ideas. In thus

ascribing to him an anachronism, there is no
intention of ignoring that the idea of the
inherent unity of all things belongs to philoso-
phies which date back many centuries before
the time of Paracelsus ; and this inexhaustible
thought contains in it the germ of so many
things that the idea of evolution as we understand it to-day may well be included therein ;
nor must it be forgotten that the theosophy
which Paracelsus professed had its own theory
of evolution ; but granting all this, these passages in " Paracelsus " have nineteenth century
writ large all over them ; and the handwriting
is the handwriting of Robert Browning :

> " Thus he dwells in all,
> From life's minute beginnings, up at last
> To man—the consummation of this scheme
> Of being, the completion of this sphere
> Of life : whose attributes had here and there
> Been scattered o'er the visible world before,
> Asking to be combined, dim fragments meant
> To be united in some wondrous whole,
> Imperfect qualities throughout creation,
> Suggesting some one creature yet to make,
> Some point where all those scattered rays should meet
> Convergent in the faculties of man.

> .   .   .   .

> Hints and previsions of which faculties
> Are strewn confusedly everywhere about

> The inferior natures, and all lead up higher,
> All shape out dimly the superior race,
> The heir of hopes too fair to turn out false,
> And man appears at last.   So far the seal
> Is put on life ; one stage of being complete,
> One scheme wound up."

But this is not all ; for since all things tend upward, man must tend upward too ; " progress is the law of life, man is not man as yet." Browning now boldly carries out the theory of evolution to its logical conclusion :—

> " But in completed man begins anew
> A tendency to God.   Prognostics told
> Man's near approach ; so in man's self arise
> August anticipations, symbols, types
> Of a dim splendour ever on before
> In that eternal circle life pursues."

A belief in this high destiny of man was the starting-point of Paracelsus, coupled with a belief that, even now, " here and there a star dispels the darkness," and isolated men arise endowed with power to raise the race :

> " Such men are even now upon the earth,
> Serene amid the half-formed creatures round
> Who should be saved by them and joined with them ; "

and he adds,—" Such was my task, and I was born to it."

It is possible that all this was not so clear to him in his youth as it was on his deathbed, looking back ; and it is certain that there were many faculties of man the value of which he fully recognised in the end, which he understood not at all at first ; but the central idea was the same.

He further believed that the divine spirit in man was hampered and clogged by the flesh ; and that many of the conditions of ordinary everyday life were incompatible with the development of man's higher, that is, his true nature. Truth, he conceived, was within man, but cloyed by these outward things ; and knowledge meant a removing of all that hid and confined truth :

> " Truth is within ourselves; it takes no rise
> From outward things, whate'er you may believe.
> There is an inmost centre in us all,
> Where truth abides in fulness; and around,
> Wall upon wall, the gross flesh hems it in,
> This perfect, clear perception—which is truth.
> A baffling and perverting carnal mesh
> Binds it, and makes all error: and to KNOW
> Rather consists in opening out a way
> Whence the imprisoned splendour may escape,
> Than in effecting entry for a light
> Supposed to be without."

Thus the problem for him who would raise
F

mankind was the problem of the flesh. "What
is this flesh we have to penetrate?" See this
soul of man, how from the cradle to the grave
it is hemmed in, now more, now less, only set
free at last by death. How often is the true
soul of a man hidden in this way from his
fellow men :

> "——One man shall crawl
> Through life surrounded with all stirring things,
> Unmoved ; and he goes mad : and from the wreck
> Of what he was, by his wild talk alone,
> You first collect how great a spirit he hid.
> Therefore, set free the soul alike in all,
> Discovering the true laws by which the flesh
> Accloys the spirit !"

This, put shortly, was the task of Paracelsus,—
*to discover the laws by which the flesh accloys the
spirit ;* and, this discovery once made, to set
free the soul of all men alike, and thus to
enable mankind to rise at one bound to its true
height :—

> "Such is my task. I go to gather this
> The sacred knowledge, here and there dispersed
> About the world, long lost or never found."

What this "sacred knowledge" was Browning
is not careful to indicate, true to the principle
which he has laid down at the start of display-

ing rather the inner workings of the soul than the agencies by which such are influenced and determined. We know, however, that the historical Paracelsus did believe in some mystical natural force, some primal essence, the secret of which was to solve the mystery of life; for, much as he despised the learning of his age, he shared the vague belief current at this time in some occult affinity between the forces of nature and the being of man,—a principle which lay at the root of the sciences of the astrologer and the alchemist; and just as the agnostic to-day breathes in at every pore the Christian spirit, his standards and ideals wholly Christian, so Paracelsus must, of necessity, have breathed the atmosphere that surrounded him. He did, in fact, study astrology and alchemy; he was initiated into the mysteries of oriental adepts; he inspected and shared the labours of Tyrolese miners; sought out wandering physicians, wise women, conjurers and empiricists of all kinds; for who could tell that the sacred knowledge might not have fallen by chance into the hands of some one—some charlatan, it might be—who, all unconscious of his priceless possession,

gave to the world wisdom's baubles, while all
the time, lying concealed in his bosom,
uncared-for and unguarded, was the pure jewel
of wisdom itself? It was however from the
direct interrogation of nature herself that
Paracelsus hoped most; and from her he
sought to wring the secret of that mystic
solvent which was, he believed, the key to
the enigma of life. But the stereotyped
dogmas of the school he despised, and
the dry learning of all those whom the
age considered sages; for was not all their
learning hitherto practically naught, since
inadequate, since all fell short of *the* knowledge which alone could serve mankind?
Therefore he must not seek the true knowledge in "one of learning's safe retreats;"
but he must go out alone, unaided by the
past, upon untrodden paths.

In all this it was the good of mankind at
large that he sought, not his own, and in man's
glory God was glorified :—

> " I never fashioned out a fancied good
> Distinct from man's ; a service to be done,
> A glory to be ministered unto
> With powers put forth at man's expense, withdrawn
> From labouring on his behalf ; a strength

Denied that might avail him. I cared not
Lest his success ran counter to success
Elsewhere : for God is glorified in man,
And to man's glory vowed I soul and limb."

The weak points in the scheme of Paracelsus were briefly these. Like the "Grammarian," he aimed high ; but, unlike the "Grammarian," he knew nothing of that view of human life which alone could reconcile him to the apparent failure which is the inevitable result of a high aim ; in virtue of which the "Grammarian," in the teeth of what men called failure, could say, —"Man has forever!" knowing well that "no work begun shall ever pause for death." "I calculated on no after-life," Paracelsus expressly states. For him there was no heaven which would complete all that was wanting here on earth ; this view of life he emphatically repudiates :—

" Mine is no mad attempt to build a world
Apart from his (God's), like those who set themselves
To find the nature of the spirit they bore,
And, taught betimes that all their gorgeous dreams
Were only born to vanish in this life,
Refused to fit them to its narrow sphere,
But chose to figure forth another world
And other frames meet for their vast desires,—
And all a dream ! Thus was life scorned ; but life
Shall yet be crowned : twine amaranth ! I am priest !"

Next, and consequent upon this, he mistook
what is "the sign and note and character of
man ;" and thought that power—power through
knowledge—was the one thing to be aimed at.
He believed that if man could only know all,
and thence have all power, he would then rise
to the height of his true destiny :—

> "——I gazed at power till I grew blind—
> Power ; I could not take my eyes from that :
> That only, I thought, should be preserved, increased
> At any risk, displayed, struck out at once—
> The sign and note and character of man."

All the sensuous and emotional side of life he
despised and neglected. Because the flesh
could hamper the spirit, he ignored the value
of flesh ; and in repudiating weakness and
sensuality, he went on to repudiate much that
goes to make up humanity. Because love, ill
conceived and ill placed, could carry in its train
much that had power to weigh the spirit down,
he rejected love ; faith, hope, and fear were
mere human weaknesses, to be shunned as he
shunned lust. He turned away from the whole
world of sense and feeling that lay around him ;—

> "—— life, death, light and shadow,
> The shows of the world, were bare receptacles

> Or indices of truth to be wrung thence,
> Not ministers of sorrow or delight ;
> A wondrous natural robe in which she went."

In spite of his pantheism, the physical world was to him only the battle-ground upon which he went forth to try his soul, the unsympathetic material from which the knowledge which he strove after was to be wrested. While he sought in the deep mines of the earth, in the mountain solitudes, for something material and tangible which would hold for him the secret of the universe, all the time the purple evenings and the dewy dawns, the shimmering summer air, were whispering the secret to him with sweet insistent voices, but in vain, for his ear was not attuned to catch the sound.

And this contempt for all those attributes of man incident to a state of imperfection carried with it a contempt for other men's work both in the past and in the present. He ignored the fact that humanity is one great whole, closely knit together, that one sows, another reaps ; one labours, another enters into his labour ; that the work of each individual is — must of necessity be — imperfect

in itself. This imperfection caused him to
estimate unfairly other men's work ; and cal-
culating men's aims from what they had
accomplished, he estimated unfairly their aims
also. The noble words of Festus found no
echo in the heart of Paracelsus :

> "———(Seek)
> Calm converse with the great dead, soul to soul,
> Who laid up treasure with the like intent
> —So lift yourself into their airy place,
> And fill out full their unfulfilled careers,
> Unravelling the knots their baffled skill
> Pronounced inextricable, true !—but left
> Far less confused. A fresh eye, a fresh hand,
> Might do much at their vigour's waning-point ;
> Succeeding with new-breathed, new-hearted force,
> As at old games the runner snatched the torch
> From runner still."

Paracelsus had no sympathy with broken
lights, with ineffectual strivings :—

> " Their light ! The sum of all is briefly this :
> They laboured and grew famous, and the fruits
> Are best seen in a dark and groaning earth
> Given over to a blind and endless strife
> With evils, what of all their lore abates?
> No ; I reject and spurn them utterly
> And all they teach. Shall I sit beside
> Their dry wells with a white and filmed eye,
> While in the distance heaven is blue above
> Mountains where sleep the unsunned tarns?"

Thus, rejecting the great past, despising his fellowmen, he isolated himself, cutting himself off from the springs of the common life of humanity.

All these mistakes sprang from a common source,—his view of the nature and purpose of this life from the cradle to the grave. This earth was to be the scene of his triumphs, as of his activities; here he was to find that which would "stay his longings vast." He sought to be satisfied here, little dreaming that satisfaction such as this would be the death of his soul. In thus making the earth his sphere, he made at the same time too great and too small demands upon this life; too great, for he sought in it that satisfaction which a season of growth and probation cannot and must not give; too small, for this life as it is, with all its hindrances and limitations, with all its evil, seemed to him wholly bad,—"a scene of degradation, ugliness, and tears, the record of disgraces best forgotten, a sullen page in human chronicles fit to erase." He required of earth that it should yield him all or nothing. He knew nothing of gain in and in virtue of opposition; did

not reflect that a tendency upward was in
itself gain, apart from any actual advance.
What earth could give him—chances of growth,
the machinery that could give his soul its true
bent; just that doubt, perplexity, longing,
pain, which give scope to the highest faculties of man, which call for faith, courage, love,
self-sacrifice,—all this he did not demand of
her, for he did not know the value of these
things. What he did demand of her, full
satisfaction for the highest aspirations of his
soul, she could not give. And further, if
she had given it, it would have been a curse
and not a blessing. For, to be satisfied here,
this, as Browning puts it elsewhere, "this is
death and the sole death;" the man who is
sufficient to himself,

> " That man has turned round on himself and stands,
>   Which in the course of nature is, to die."

This was the lesson which life was to teach
Paracelsus. For he was out of harmony with
the conditions under which he lived. The man
who despises life here on earth, because he
has seen the Beatific Vision, and, like Lazarus
in " Karshish," cannot henceforward properly
estimate the things of earth, has a consistent

philosophy of life; the man who says,—"Eat, drink, be merry; to-morrow we die!" has the same. Paracelsus combined the antagonistic elements in both views; for, while looking for no after-life, he despised this life. True, the secret once his, in perfected humanity here on earth he would have found the missing note; but until and unless this was found, all was discord and confusion.

Meantime, none the less brightly gleamed in the distance the golden pinnacles of the city of his dreams and his desires; and with burning faith and steadfast will he set out confident of reaching it one day.

II.

Paracelsus at Basil.

" Love's undoing taught me the worth of love in
man's estate."

PARACELSUS met Aprile at a turning-point
in his life.   He stood then where two ways
met, and Aprile it was who determined his
course.   Nine years had passed since he set
out with such indomitable confidence,—nine
years, and the way had been long and
stubborn.   Now, though still young, he
found himself with " grey hair, faded hands,
and furrowed brow."   He had gone on with
his eyes so intent upon the distant goal that
he had not noticed before how little progress
he had made, and how time was passing.
The accident of his going to the house of
the Greek astrologer at Constantinople first
awoke him to the consciousness of this.
For this man required of Paracelsus, as of

all who came to him for help, that he
should note down in a book especially kept
for such records, all that he had attained to
up to this, the plain hard facts, just the
knowledge, practical, tangible, that he had
acquired. There was to be no filling up of
the blanks by

" A brilliant future to supply and perfect
All half-gains and conjectures and crude hopes ; "

nothing was to be recorded except that
actually gained. And what had he written?
A few blurred characters sufficed to record—
practically nothing. He had wandered through
many lands, and had made a few isolated
discoveries, valueless in themselves, mere
fragments of truth ; and there they lay,
all in " a dim heap, fact and surmise together
confusedly massed ; "

" And yet these blottings chronicle a life—
A whole life, and my life ! "

He now stood face to face with a fact
that in his confident youth he must
indeed have known, but that he had not
taken into account, and yet the most obvious
and universal of all facts ;—life on earth is

limited, and man's physical powers are limited.
There it was, facing him, standing and blocking
the way. He had nothing to reproach himself
with in his pursuit of the end which he had
set before him. He had not "gone slightingly
through his task;" he had subdued his life
beyond the obligation of his strictest vow,
given his nature up,

> "——Consenting fully
> All passionate impulses its soil was formed
> To rear, should wither;"

his renunciation of love and all the softer
elements in ·life was now more complete than
it had been nine years before; for his pursuit
of knowledge had developed in him still
further a "wolfish hunger after knowledge"
much more absorbing than even the craving of
his youth had been; and yet he had not
reached the goal; he had made no appreciable
advance towards it; and his physical powers
were failing. And now a miserable doubt
comes. Has he been wholly right in this
fruitless renunication of all human joys?
Thoughts of Festus, of Michal and the loves
of his youth, crowd in upon him, caressingly,
appealingly. Surely, if God's sun has shone

on his pursuit of knowledge, "o'er that happy
strip a sun shone too;"

> "And fainter gleams it as the waves grow rough,
> And still more faint as the sea widens; last
> I sicken on a dead gulf streaked with light
> From its own putrefying depths alone.
> Then, God was pledged to take me by the hand;
> Now, any miserable juggle can bid
> My pride depart."

And there is a lower depth still which opens
out under his feet, a deeper curse. Worse than
failure, worse than the weariness of the baffled
fighter, the loss of youth and his brave hopes,
is the horrible suggestion,—have his aims
remained pure as ever? has he kept his primal
light from waning? why is it that he cannot
wish that, though he sink, some other may
succeed?

> "O God, the despicable heart of us!
> Shut out this hideous mockery from my heart!"

Thus, exhausted, perplexed, doubting, despairing, what can he do next? First the idea of
rest holds him, and, once entertained, quickly
gains ground. How good to dare let down
the high-strung brain, to unnerve the harassed,

over-taxed frame.   But soon he gathers
strength, and casts the thought from him :—

> " No, no, there needs not this ; no, after all,
> At worst I have performed my share of the task ;
> The rest is God's concern ; mine, merely this,
> To know that I have obstinately held
> By my own work. The mortal, whose brave foot
> Has trod, unscathed, the temple court so far
> That he descries at length the shrine of shrines,
> Must let no sneering of the demons' eyes,
> Whom he could pass, unquailing, fasten now
> Upon him, fairly past their power ; no, no——
> He must not stagger, faint, fall down at last,
> Having a charm to baffle them ; behold,
> He bares his front : a mortal ventures thus
> Serene amid the echoes, beams, and glooms !
> If he be priest henceforth, if he wake up
> The god of the place to ban and blast him there,
> Both well ! What's failure or success to me ?
> I have subdued my life to the one purpose
> Whereto I ordained it ; there alone I spy ;
> No doubt, that way I may be satisfied."

But how go on ? He has fed " a fire meant
to hold out till morn arrived with inexhaustible
light," and " lo, I have heaped my last, and
day dawns not."

It is at this point, when to stop and when
to go on seem alike impossible, that he meets
Aprile ; and Aprile pours into his ears his
gospel of love—love—love. Aprile too has
missed the goal ; but his aim was not that of

Paracelsus, nor were their weak points the same. " I would love infinitely, and be loved," is his own statement of his aim. He has in short seen only too well the exceeding value of all that Paracelsus has despised and neglected. He has bathed himself, lost himself, in "the loveliness of life." The beauty of the robe, that wondrous garment in which truth clothes herself so as to be visible to mortal eye, that robe which Paracelsus could not see for straining after the vision of the form which it clothed, was to Aprile all-sufficient. He had failed to learn that knowledge must go hand in hand with love ; and that to realise in its fulness even the frailest joy, there must be earnest endeavour and patient toil. But unlike as he was to Paracelsus, and unlike as his aim had been, he nevertheless resembled Paracelsus in this, that he too failed to realise that he must work within life's limitations, never satisfied, but never despairing. He had gazed presumptuously on the face of beauty herself, and nothing less could satisfy him. He could not carry out the petty task of embodying imperfectly one small fraction of beauty, and giving it to the world, while all around him

G

shapes innumerable pressed, dazzling him, blinding him, visions of beauty which no means within his reach could adequately represent. And now, in spite of his rich endowments, gifts bestowed on him to be used in the service of his fellow men, he is dying, having accomplished nothing. But at the last the primal light waxes only the brighter. Failure has begotten in him no doubt as to the value of that which he has aimed at. Too much love was his undoing ; and yet, with no uncertain voice, but unhesitatingly, emphatically, he asserts the end of life to be love.

And to Paracelsus love's undoing, in the case of Aprile, first teaches " the use of love in man's estate." Thus must the years have thrown much light for him on the significance of failure. Aprile dying because blinded by love and the loveliness of life, only serves to show to Paracelsus the exceeding value of all the sensuous side of life, of all that he has neglected. Not that it shakes his faith in his own aim ; rather they are the two parts of a dissevered world,—parts which God has joined together here on earth, in indissoluble union, and which Paracelsus and Aprile had both tried to rend asunder.

The direct result of the influence of Aprile upon Paracelsus was that he now determined to work while he had the light, " for the night cometh ; " and to give his gains, all meagre and imperfect as they were, to the world. Later he describes this passage in his life to Festus. Just at this time a passionate regret for youth and health and love so vainly lavished was foremost in his thoughts ;

" ———and this strange fact
Humbled me wondrously, and had due force
In rendering me the less averse to follow
A certain counsel, a mysterious warning—
You will not understand—but 't was a man
With aims not mine and yet pursued like mine,
With the same fervour and no more success,
Perishing in my sight ; who summoned me
As I would shun the ghastly fate I saw,
To serve my race at once ; to wait no longer
That God should interfere on my behalf,
But to distrust myself, put pride away,
And give my gains, imperfect as they were,
To men."

For this was the lesson that Aprile's own wasted life had taught him :—

" ———Nay, listen,
Knowing ourselves, our world, our task so great,
Our time so brief, 't is clear if we refuse
The means so limited, the tools so rude

To execute our purpose, life will fleet,
And we shall fade, and leave our task undone.
We will be wise in time : ”

Paracelsus now determines to profit by this warning. Since he can never do all that he once hoped to do, he will at least do that which lies within his power. To this end he now accepts the chair of medicine at the University of Basil.

Here he enters upon a life entirely new, and one for which all that has gone before has in no wise fitted him. For his real knowledge is vast, shadowy, incommunicable ; while the empirical knowledge, scraps, odds and ends, the few secrets that he has acquired by the way, form no consistent scheme, and yet they are all that he can give to the world. But just this knowledge was received with enthusiasm by his hearers. The age was not scientific ; and certain real discoveries in chemistry, as well as certain real cures effected by him, soon won for him a reputation that made him feel strong enough to attack openly all the systems of medicine that had preceded him. For this he was applauded both by those to whom his cures seemed marvellous and also by those in

whom the spirit of revolt was strong; and
soon we find the theatre at Basil thronged
with eager students who press round the new
master,—

> " The wondrous Paracelsus, life's dispenser,
> Fate's commissary, idol of the schools
> And courts."

With all this a new pitfall opened out
under his feet, one least expected by him,
and against which he was least on his guard.
Who could have dreamed that he, who
despised anything which fell short of the one
true knowledge, absolute and complete, could
be flattered by this homage paid to knowledge which he knew was in itself valueless?
He, who had gazed at the true wisdom full
in the face, how could he have foreseen that
he could ever descend to posing as a wonder-
worker, because he was in possession of a
few chemical secrets which so far the rest of
the world knew nothing of?   It was a profound student of human nature who once
said,—" Be on your guard against that fault
which you think you are most free from."
Paracelsus seems to have succumbed to the
unexpectedness and the suddenness of the

onslaught. The transition from the weary, fruitless searching for the unattainable to rest —a resting upon that gained, however small, —from the constant, grinding sense of failure to the atmosphere of eager recognition, must have brought balm to the weary spirit ; and the flowery path in the valley once entered upon, it was hard to return to the arid desert or the rugged mountain side. But the man who "pressed God's lamp close to his breast" could not rest upon this. He might sink, but he could not sink and be happy. The picture of Paracelsus at Basil presents a psychological study of the deepest interest, crowded with apparent inconsistencies, but for this reason all the more true to human nature, a study in which cross lights meet and seem to clash, while now this, now that side of a many-sided nature presents itself.

One prominent point to notice is that the influence of Aprile in urging upon him the part which love ought to play, and does in fact play, in human life, has acted only partially and ineffectively. He had seen with a sudden flash his own deep error in ignoring all this side of life, and had quickly deter-

mined to live differently.   But to give one's
life an .entirely new bent is a thing easier
to resolve upon than to carry through ;
nor is it always a safe or a wise thing
to endeavour to *sortir de son génie*.   Paracelsus and Aprile had each of them a
distinct individuality, which neither could
escape from.   God speaks with many voices
to many men.   He had spoken to Aprile
through the loveliness of life ; he had spoken
to Paracelsus in visions of the night.   The
voice was one, but the form in which each
heard it bore the impress of the personality
of each.   There is an indescribable pathos in
the words with which Paracelsus describes his
efforts to give his life this new bent :—

> "God ! how I essayed
> To live like that mad poet, for a while,
> To love alone ; and how I felt too warped
> And twisted and deformed ! .   .   .
> .   .   .   .
> I cannot feed on beauty for the sake
> Of beauty only, nor can drink in balm
> From lovely objects for their loveliness ;
> My nature cannot lose her first imprint ;
> I must still hoard and heap and class all truths
> With one ulterior purpose : I must know !
> Would God translate me to his throne, believe
> That I should only listen to his word

To further my own aim ! For other men,
Beauty is prodigally strewn around,
And I were happy could I quench as they
This mad and thriveless longing, and content me
With beauty for itself alone : alas !
I have addressed a frock of heavy mail,
Yet may not join the troop of sacred knights ;
And now the forest creatures fly from me,
The grass-banks cool, the sunbeams warm no more."

He feels that he has lived for knowledge and
failed ; that he has tried to live for love, and
failed ; thus he is betrayed by both. He is
experiencing all the worse effects of following
the advice of Aprile, and none of the better.
He has curbed his spirit's flight, and consented
to fill "the petty circle lotted out of infinite
space," which is all that life here at Basil
offers to him, and yet he cannot live the
ordinary life of ordinary men and women—
loving, fearing, hoping, trusting ; and he cannot
love these men whom he feels to be so far
beneath him, and in whom love shows itself
in a form so different from his conception of
what it ought to be. For he has entered
upon the thought of Aprile with the same
headlong impetuosity which has always characterised him. He understands no compromise.
If love is all, love must be pure and strong,

or it is worthless; and because he cannot see that it is this in any of his fellow-men, he rejects it utterly in them.

And now the lower consolations incident to such a life become clamorous, and he is not deaf to their voices. While despising the adulation which he received, he yet likes it and encourages it, having so far fallen away from his once proud attitude as to feel that, since he can no longer look for the true recompense, he may at least accept those crumbs by the way, due to him from a world that he has used himself up in serving. And there is a lower depth still; for the claims of the flesh which he seems to have crucified in vain, now become urgent. Now that he has found out that that for which he has foregone all youthful appetites is unattainable, the low thought suggests itself,—at least why not enjoy? If the highest satisfaction, if true happiness is impossible, pleasure, at least, is always within one's reach:

> " Yet, I deny not, there is made provision
> Of joys which tastes less jaded might affect;
> Nay, some which please me too, for all my pride—
> Pleasures that once were pains: the iron ring
> Festering about a slave's neck grows at length
> Into the flesh it eats. I no longer hate

> A host of petty vile delights, undreamed of
> Or spurned before; such now supply the place
> Of my dead aims: as in the autumn woods
> Where tall trees used to flourish, from their roots
> Springs up a fungus brood sickly and pale,
> Chill mushrooms coloured like a corpse's cheek."

Thus he is incapable of sharing in the higher joys of actual flesh and blood existence, while the lower hold him in thrall.

And through all this the light burns bright. He never deceives himself. He knows that all his outward success is degradation: "As though here did not signify defeat!" he retorts with impatience to Festus, good, simple Festus, who sees in the high position of Paracelsus at Basil just all that he has longed for and dreamed of for him; and who, when Paracelsus talks of defeat, urges—"Still I find you here!' as an incontrovertible proof of success. Paracelsus has no such illusions; no apparent success blinds him for a moment. It is not so much that these people praise him for powers that he does not really possess, it is that, even if he possessed them, there is still the break-down of his general aims, a failure in him to reach that for which God intended him. It is the ever-present sense of this, the

imperishable power of his boyhood's vision, that
keeps him from the lowest depth of all :—

> " After all, Festus, you say well : I am
> A man yet : I need never humble me.
> I would have been—something, I know not what ;
> But though I cannot soar, I do not crawl.
> There are worse portions than this one of mine.
> You say well ! . . and deeper degradation !
> If the mean stimulants of vulgar praise,
> If vanity should become the chosen food
> Of a sunk mind, should stifle even the wish
> To find its early aspirations true,
> Should teach it to breathe falsehood like life-breath—
> An atmosphere of craft and trick and lies ;
> Should make it proud to emulate, surpass
> Base natures in the practices which woke
> Its most indignant loathing once . . . No, no !
> Utter damnation is reserved for hell !
> I had immortal feelings ; such shall never
> Be wholly quenched : no, no ! "

Why then does he remain at Basil ? one asks
with Festus. For many different, almost conflicting reasons. It is really a counsel of
despair. His earliest aims are unattainable ;
the new life for love has proved itself impossible ; here, at worst, he does " most good
and least harm ; " and here he is not wholly
cut off from his old dreams ; " their faint
ghosts can sit and flatter him, and send him
back content to his dull round." He cannot,

it is true, join the band of sacred knights;
but still he may "follow, dreaming that ere
night arrive he will o'ertake the company,
and ride glittering as they." It is this hope,
the hope that he may one day aspire again,
may one day enter again upon the life he
has left which alone sustains him now, alone
saves him from sinking beyond recall. And
here he is doing, if not all that he hoped
when he first adopted Aprile's advice, at
least something; he is teaching what he can,
meagre as it is. He is not doing it well,
because his life's training has not taught him
how to impart knowledge; and his "uncouth
habits," his " small skill to speak," his
"impatient spirit" render him ill-fitted to be a
teacher; but, well or ill, he is working for other
men. Even this, however, affords him but little
satisfaction, while it is a continual occasion of
stumbling to him. For the only knowledge
which he can impart is not his best:—

> " I possess
> Two kinds of knowledge ;—one—vast, shadowy,
> Hints of the unbounded aim I once possessed ;
> The other consists of many secrets, caught
> While bent on nobler prize, perhaps a few
> Prime principles which may conduct to much.
> These last I offer to my followers here."

But just these secrets are what the vulgar voice exaggerates into miraculous powers; hence the temptation to vanity, deceit, and all the degrading depths that follow.

Thus is the tortured soul torn asunder by conflicting forces ;—his old aims ever beckoning to him in the distance ; the flagging body ever present with its monotonous, iron-tongued rejoinder,—" Thus far shalt thou go, and no further ; " the lower gratifications both of mind and body ever within his reach ; and the lower impulses within him too strong to be continually repressed, since repression avails nothing towards his old ends ; and through it all the consciousness that he has missed much in life that can never be regained for the sake of that which he will never attain to.

And yet what an incalculable advance in insight he has made since, a boy of nineteen, he first looked out upon the world. The pain and turmoil of the last few years have wrested some secrets from life which the boy's keen eyes, gazing far afield, had overlooked. He is slowly but inevitably learning this lesson, that no man lives to himself,—learning how a man may best live his life in a world where " we

see through a glass, darkly." His first proud
impulse was to see all, to know all. Well, he
has gone out, he has striven his bravest; and
yet he does not see; and the power that is
stronger than he is none the less strong for
that. Further, he now realises that he will
never know with that perfect knowledge which
alone can be a sure guide, if knowledge is to
be the guide at all; and with this conviction
comes, as it must come, a realisation that not
knowledge is the especial mark of man at his
highest; that man, being imperfect, and living
in a world where perfect knowledge is impossible, must seek his being's true harmony some
other way :

> "Were man all mind, he gains
> A station little enviable. From God
> Down to the lowest spirit ministrant,
> Intelligence exists which casts our mind
> Into immeasurable shade."

It is true that "the imperious thinking power"
still holds him in thrall, because he cannot
free himself; but he knows that it is thraldom;
and he knows that this way he can never be
satisfied. He is realising in his own life the
workings of a truth which he has always
recognised. For he has always known that

if God, for his own good purpose, does
separate "man's pin-point rock of love and
power" from his own "boundless continent,"
yet that the rock and the continent are one;
but, in spite of this, he has isolated himself,
and lived self-centred and self-dependent; and
instead of looking upon himself as one member
of an innumerable company, all deriving a
common life from the one eternal source of
life, he has aspired to stand alone and in his
own right to know. Such a man may indeed
live in the world, but he has cut himself off
from the springs of life. There is no truer
truth than just this,—the meek shall inherit
the earth. Those who have best realised their
dependence, and who live their lives recognising
their true relationship to God and to their
fellow-men, to them does this life yield its
best. For these two things go together. The
higher a man rises towards the one eternal
source of life, the more does he respect the
weakest signs of life in his fellow-men, knowing
well whence it springs. It is he who has
separated his own light from the boundless
sea of light around him who despises the half-
lights of others. This Paracelsus now knows,

although he cannot act upon it; and since knowledge is dethroned from its high place, all the other essentially human attributes assert their claim,—love, by which the being of a man goes out, reaches beyond itself, giving itself to, and thus possessing all things—that which binds all the world in one, as the calm ether binds the stars together; hope, which makes the darkness bright; fear, which warns a man at noon-day that the night comes; faith, which gives sight to the blind,—

> " Love, hope, fear, faith,—these make humanity ;
> These are its sign and note and character."

These, the essential conditions of a state of training and probation, are the faculties in the possession and exercise of which alone a man can place himself in harmony with the rest of the universe ; and he who attempts to lift himself above them runs counter to all the forces which are at work around him.

And the recognition of this carries with it for Paracelsus a juster estimate of his own work and that of others. He still knows that he is one of those especially dowered for an especial task ; but the conviction that he himself, in this short

life, will never complete that task, causes him
to look with new eyes upon the imperfect work
of other men, and enables him to assign to
himself his true place and rank among them :

    " Come, I will show you where my merit lies.
     'Tis in the advance of individual minds
     That the slow crowd should gain their expectation
     Eventually to follow ; as the sea
     Waits ages in its bed till some one wave
     Out of the multitudinous mass, extends
     The empire of the whole, some feet perhaps,
     Over the strip of sand which could confine
     Its fellows so long time : thenceforth the rest,
     Even to the meanest, hurry in at once,
     And so much is clear gained. I shall be glad
     If all my labours, failing of aught else,
     Suffice to make such inroad and procure
     A wider range for thought : nay, they do this ;
     For, whatsoe'er my notions of true knowledge
     And a legitimate success, may be,
     I am not blind to my undoubted rank
     When classed with others : I precede my age :
     And whoso wills is very free to mount
     These labours as a platform whence his own
     May have a prosperous outset."

Thus far has he advanced since the time when
he "rejected and spurned utterly " the work of
other men ; and when later, in the astrologer's
cell, he could not wish that, though he failed,
some other might succeed. He does not deny
his own rich endowments ; he knows that he

H

can go further than other men, but only as one
wave of the sea can go some feet further than
its fellows; and he knows that an age which
shall succeed him will go further than he.

But all this knowledge gained by experience
lies confusedly heaped together. It has not
so far grouped itself into a consistent scheme
of life that can be acted upon. To Paracelsus
now one, now another aspect of the truth has
presented itself, but the whole lacks cohesion
and rounding off; and the lesson is not yet
learned until all shall have been woven into
a consistent whole, and applied to practical,
every-day life. His state of mind when he
was at last driven from Basil, exposed as a
quack, followed by the scorn of those who
a short time before had extolled him as a
god, shows how little practical effect all this
new light had upon him. The strongest
and most absorbing feeling in his soul was
hatred of those whose stupidity had failed to
recognise all that was true in him. For it
was when he tried to be true that they rejected
him:

> "Just so long as I was pleased
> To play off the mere antics of my art,
> Fantastic gambols leading to no end,

I got huge praise : but one can ne'er keep down
Our foolish nature's weakness.   There they flocked,
Poor devils, jostling, swearing, and perspiring,
Till the walls rang again ; and all for me !
I had a kindness for them, which was right ;
But then I stopped not till I tacked to that
A trust in them and a respect—a sort
Of sympathy for them ; I must needs begin
To teach them, not amaze them, ' to impart
'The spirit which should instigate the search
'Of truth,' just what you bade me !   I spoke out.
Forthwith a mighty squadron, in disgust,
Filed off."

There is little trace here of any respect for
the half-lights of others ; it is difficult to feel
that he recognises these men as in any way
his fellows.   He himself shudders before the
picture which his heart, filled with contempt
and hatred, presents at this time :—

"Festus, were your nature fit
To be defiled, your eyes the eyes to ache
At gangrene-blotches, eating poison-blains,
The ulcerous barky scurf of leprosy
Which finds—a man, and leaves—a hideous thing
That cannot but be mended by hell-fire,
—I would lay bare to you the human heart
Which God cursed long ago, and devils make since
Their pet nest and their never-tiring home.
Oh, sages have discovered we are born
For various ends—to love, to know : has ever
One stumbled, in his search, on any signs
Of a nature in us formed to hate ?   To hate ?

> If that be our true object which evokes
> Our powers in fullest strength, be sure 't is hate !
> Yet men have doubted if the best and bravest
> Of spirits can nourish him with hate alone.
> I had not the monopoly of fools,
> It seems, at Basil."

And now that he is setting out again in the pursuit of his old aims, though not by the old means, in seeming to retain all that was good in his earliest scheme while rejecting all that was mistaken, there is still no harmonious whole, but rather a confused mass of conflicting beliefs and impulses. The old fire is still there, but also the old despair that followed. Further, the casting aside of the narrowing asceticism of his youth has caused him to forget the fact that in all true effort asceticism plays its part ; or, if he still recognises this, passions and lower impulse once set loose refuse now to return to bondage. He states his scheme thus :—

> " This is my plan . . . .
> I will accept all helps ; all I despised
> So rashly at the outset, equally
> With early impulses, late years have quenched :
> I have tried each way singly : now for both !
> All helps ! no one sort shall exclude the rest.
> I seek to know and to enjoy at once,
> Not one without the other as before.
> Suppose my labour should seem God's own cause

Once more, as I first dreamed,—it shall not baulk me
Of the meanest, earthliest, sensualest delight
That may be snatched ; for every joy is gain,
And gain is gain, however small. My soul
Can die then, nor be taunted—'what was gained?'
Nor, on the other hand, should pleasure follow
As though I had not spurned her hitherto,
Shall she o'ercloud my spirit's rapt communion
With the tumultuous past, the teeming future,
Glorious with visions of a full success."

But that this plan had not in it the elements
of success is abundantly shown by its working
while he was still at Basil. Nothing could
better describe the many different elements
which went to make up his life there than
these following words to Festus ; and the
whole is one great discord :—

" And Festus quits me
To give place to some credulous disciple
Who holds that God is wise, but Paracelsus
Has his peculiar merits : I suck in
That homage, chuckle o'er that admiration,
And then dismiss the fool ; for night is come,
And I betake myself to study again,
Till patient strivings after hidden lore
Half wring some bright truth from its prison ; my frame
Trembles, my forehead's veins swell out, my hair
Tingles for triumph.   Slow and sure the morn
Shall break on my pent room and dwindling lamp
And furnace dead, and scattered earths and ores ;
When, with a failing heart and throbbing brow,

I must review my captured truth, sum up
Its value, trace what ends to what begins,
Its present power with its eventual bearings,
Latent affinities, the views it opens,
And its full length in perfecting my scheme.
I view it sternly circumscribed, cast down
From the high place my fond hopes yielded it,
Proved worthless—which, in getting, yet had cost
Another wrench to this fast-falling frame.
Then, quick, the cup to quaff, that chases sorrow,
I lapse back into youth, and take again
My fluttering pulse for evidence that God
Means good to me, will make my cause his own."

What is it that is still lacking? Why cannot he act upon the knowledge gained, and add his little gains to those of the past, hoping for the future? With so much light why is the whole so dark and discordant? Is there no reason deeper than the force of old training, old habits? There is one truth which he has not yet realised so far that it forms any vital part of his scheme of life, and yet it is that which gives a meaning, gives cohesion to the whole. For life, even when the true relationships of things are duly recognised, is still meaningless if the grave ends it. Paracelsus up to this had " calculated on no after-life ; " and even now a wondering, hesitating sense of life beyond the

grave has only just begun to arise in his
soul, unbidden.   Hearing of Michal's death,
he gives expression to this :

> " Now, do you know,
> I can reveal a secret which shall comfort
> Even you.   I have no julep, as men think,
> To cheat the grave ; but a far better secret.
> Know, then, you did not ill to trust your love
> To the cold earth : I have thought much of it :
> For I believe we do not wholly die.
>   . . . Nay, do not laugh ; there is a reason
> For what I say : I think the soul can never
> Taste death.   I am, just now, as you may see,
> Very unfit to put so strange a thought
> In an intelligible dress of words ;
> But take it as my trust, she is not dead."

It is not the death of a beloved friend which
forces this thought in upon his soul, as might
have been the case with a weaker man ; it is
the lesson of life's experience.   All that he
has learned up to this is incomplete and of
little value without this.   For, in truth it is
in the light of this alone that many of the
conditions of human life, as lived here on
earth, gain a meaning, and show a purpose.
It cannot be denied that in some a vivid
realisation of a future life has bred a contempt
for this ; but they are the truer and the deeper

thinkers who know that it is only in the light
of a future that we can say of this life,—" it
means intensely, and means good." When
once Paracelsus recognised the value of those
attributes of man which have no meaning or
use unless life is a probation-time, the sense
of a fuller life somewhere, at some time, must
have been in the background. But his
apologetic tone to Festus,—" nay, do not
laugh,"—shows how new and strange the
thought was put into words and assuming a
definite form. One can picture the perplexity
of Festus, the man of unshaken orthodoxy, on
finding that this, one of the most elementary
articles of his creed, has only just begun to
dawn upon the " mighty, majestic spirit " of
his friend. Festus, walking in the old, beaten
track, accepting without understanding, stands
in the end hand in hand with the storm-tossed
soul which sees at last, the conviction driven
in by hard fact upon a brain that thinks and
questions and weighs.

III.

PARACELSUS ATTAINS.

"My foot is on the threshold of boundless life."

WHEN we next see Paracelsus, thirteen years
have passed since he left Basil, and he is dying. His "varied life," with all its storms and
struggles, its aspirations, vain triumphs and
defeats, "drifts by him," and now that it is
past he first understands it all. What he
failed to learn by "the happy, prompt, instinctive way of youth," the years, "exacting their
accompt of pain," have taught him, and taught
him well. He who in his proud youth esteemed
a place among the proudest of the earth not
supportable; who felt, when human effort rose
highest, that he must elevate himself "far, far
above the gorgeous spectacle," is now content to
take his place with the lowliest of mankind :—

" .   .   . Lay me,
When I shall die, within some narrow grave,
Not by itself—for that would be too proud—

But where such graves are thickest ; let it look
Nowise distinguished from the hillocks round,
So that the peasant at his brother's bed
May tread upon my own, and know it not ;
And we shall all be equal at the last."

The failure of his own efforts, his own weakness, his own sin, in spite of what he knows
to have been his own true light, have taught
him to estimate fairly the failures and imperfections of other men; have led him to the
knowledge of the meaning and use of all
human limitations, and to that further knowledge, the last link in the chain, the knowledge
of the true significance of that portion of
life which lasts from the cradle to the grave.
Now dying, outcast and disgraced, in the
eyes of all the world most miserable, for-
saken by all except his one friend Festus,
who watches in love and loyalty beside his
bed, he triumphs as he never triumphed before.
All the scattered shreds of knowledge which
the years have brought him, all the broken
lights which have shone upon him, now bright,
now dim, as, now with flying feet, now weary
and footsore, he trod the path of life, are
gathered into one; and lo, in the dark cell in

the hospital of St. Sebastian, it is bright
noonday!

> "Where'er I look is fire, where'er I listen
> Music, and where I tend bliss evermore."

"Tell me but this," Festus asks him, "You are
not in despair?"

Paracelsus.   I?   For what?
Festus.   Alas, alas! he knows not, as I feared!
Paracelsus. What is it that you ask me with that earnest,
             Dear, searching face?
Festus.   How feel you, Aureole?
Paracelsus.   Well:
             Well.

Yes, it is well with him. He is dying, and
thinner and thinner has grown the veil which
hides the great unseen from the eyes of
sense:

> "And this is death: I understand it all.
> New being waits me; new perceptions must
> Be born in me before I plunge therein;
> Which last is Death's affair; and while I speak,
> Minute by minute he is filling me
> With power, and while my foot is on the threshold
> Of boundless life—the doors unopened yet,
> All preparations not complete within—
> I turn new knowledge upon old events."

He now looks upon a future life as something
so inevitable, so self-evident, that he no longer

states his belief in it as a conclusion, nor comments upon it in any way, as a scientist never stops to prove the heat of the sun to those who live by its rays. And this full realisation of the wider sphere upon which he is entering, so far from making him underrate the importance of earthly life, has the opposite effect ; for the same light which illumines for him life beyond the grave, illumines also each back step in the life that is behind him, and the whole meaning of all that has been dark before opens out before him. Now that he at last realises the meaning of life, he realises the meaning of imperfection.

A perfectly clear and logically consistent principle lay at the root of the belief of Paracelsus all through. He could not acquiesce in the idea of imperfection as the ultimate stage of the human race ; his reason, as well as his moral instinct, refused to rest upon the thought. He rejected it as something lawless, irrational, impossible. So long as he hoped for a perfected humanity here on earth, he looked for no afterlife, because this life gave him all that he demanded. So soon as he learned in the hard school of experience that this hope was vain, then the conviction was forced upon him that

this was not the end. And the belief in a
future life once his, all his life behind him
assumed a meaning that it never had before.
For it is certain that one makes totally different
demands upon life according as one looks upon
it as the ultimate goal or as a training ground
in which the soul is fitted for its " adventure
brave and new " beyond the grave. Limitations
which are intolerable looked at in the one light,
become more than tolerable, they assume a use
and a purpose, when looked at in the other. It
was when he knew that earth was not the goal
that the idea of earth as a place of probation
gathered force ; and a different light was cast
upon hindrances of all kinds as soon as they
were looked upon as " machinery just meant to
give the soul its bent ; " a different light was
cast upon his own failures, as well as the
failures of other men, when once he knew that
" no work begun shall ever pause for death."
It is true that he might have so looked upon
human limitations, seen the same " gain by
opposition " as leading up to perfection here
on earth ; but his idea had been that the
race was to rise to its true height all at
once ; there was no room in his scheme for

a gradual progress.   The liberation of man
was to have been a work altogether outside
the individual ;   each man took no part, so
to speak, in his own salvation.   It was only
in the light of the after-life that he seems
to have seen that " man shall painfully attain
to joy ; " and that as a man struggles so
does he attain.

But all this new knowledge only makes
the vision of his youth stand out the clearer.
Looking back he knows now " that rage was
right i' the main, that acquiescence vain."
True the reflex light from his deathbed
reveals to him now for the first time what
was the full significance of that " fierce
energy " of his early days, " striving because
its nature was to strive ; " what he had seen
confusedly then he now sees clearly ; many
things that he had not seen at all then form
a vital part of his philosophy of life now ;
but the first use he makes of this fuller
knowledge is to ratify the vision of his
youth, and to declare with no uncertain voice
that it was a true light that shone upon him
then.   Throughout his proud youth, his
humbled manhood, and now on his triumphant

deathbed, there is the same pathetic insistence upon this :—

> " ———Festus, from childhood I have been possessed
> By a fire, by a true fire, or faint or fierce,
> As from without some master, so it seemed,
> Repressed or urged its current."

This was the faith with which he started ;
and now he recalls as his best, truest moment,
"that happy time when he first vowed himself
to man." He now knows that in youth he
stood already at that point which many men
spend a lifetime in reaching ; and that he
was thus especially endowed because he was
given an especial task to do :—

> " Yes, it was in me ; I was born for it,—
> I, Paracelsus ; it was mine by right.
> Doubtless a searching and impetuous soul
> Might learn from its own motions that some task
> Like this awaited it about the world ;
> Might seek somewhere in this blank life of ours
> For fit delights to stay its longings vast ;
> And, grappling nature, so prevail on her
> To fill the creature full she dared thus frame
> Hungry for joy ; and, bravely tyrannous,
> Grow in demand, still craving more and more,
> And make each joy conceded prove a pledge
> Of other joy to follow—bating nought
> Of its desires, still seizing fresh pretence
> To turn the knowledge and the rapture wrung
> As an extreme, last boon, from destiny,

> Into occasion for new covetings,
> New strifes, new triumphs ; doubtless a strong soul,
> Alone unaided might attain to this ;
>
> .   .   .   .
> But this was born in me; I was made so."

But if the light which blessed his youth now blends with the light which crowns his death-bed, so that the whole stands out in dazzling radiance ; if he now sees as he never saw before how deep are the wells from which it springs, how high the heavens which cannot contain it, its brightness shows him all the more his own deep errors, shows him the clouds which from time to time had obscured the light and betrayed him into strange by-ways :—

> "This is my case :
> If I go joyous back to God, yet bring
> No offering, if I render up my soul
> Without the fruits it was ordained to bear,
> If I appear the better to love God
> For sin, as one who has no claim on him,—
> Be not deceived ! It may be surely thus
> With me, while higher prizes still await
> The mortal persevering to the end."

He now sees as he never saw before, not even when it was first revealed to him by Aprile's fate, his own mistake in trying to separate the eternal truth towards which his soul went out in yearning from the lowliest manifestation of

it here on earth; as in those days when he
thought that power, and power alone, was to
be aimed at; when he despised mankind and
despised the past, all because of imperfections
and weakness :—

"I saw no use in the past, only a scene
Of degradation, ugliness and tears,
The record of disgraces best forgotten,
A sullen page in human chronicles
Fit to erase. I saw no cause why man
Should not stand all-sufficient even now,
Or why his annals should be forced to tell
That once the tide of light, about to break
Upon the world, was sealed within its spring;
I would have had one day, one moment's space,
Change man's condition, push each slumbering claim
Of mastery o'er the elemental world
At once to full maturity, then roll
Oblivion o'er the work, and hide from man
What night had ushered morn."

But as the years passed and the morning did
not dawn, life was teaching him her lessons :—

"   .   .   .   As one by one
My dreams grew dim, my wide aims circumscribed,
As actual good within my reach decreased,
While obstacles sprang up this way and that,
To keep me from effecting half the sum,
Small as it proved; as objects, mean within
The primal aggregate, seemed, even the least,
Itself a match for my concentred strength—
What wonder if I saw no way to shun
Despair?"

I

Then it was that the fate of Aprile spoke to
him :—

> " ——Love's undoing
> Taught me the worth of love in man's estate,
> And what proportion love should hold with power
> In his right constitution ; love preceding
> Power, and with much power, always much more love ;
> Love still too straitened in his present means,
> And earnest for new power to set love free."

But even then the whole was not learned. If
he admitted the importance of other human
attributes a swell as power, he looked for those
attributes in a state of perfection. He had
yet to learn that as power, though not put forth
blindly, cannot yet be controlled by perfect
knowledge, but must be " used at risk, inspired
or checked by hope and fear ;" as knowledge is
not all intuition, as he once thought, but " the
slow uncertain fruit of an enhancing toil,
strengthened by love ;" so even love itself is

> " ——not serenely pure,
> But strong from weakness, like a chance-sown plant,
> Which, cast on stubborn soil, puts forth changed buds
> And softer stains, unknown in happier climes ;
> Love which endures and doubts and is oppressed
> And cherished, suffering much and much sustained,
> And blind, oft-failing, yet believing love,
> A half-enlightened, often chequered trust."

Paracelsus had no tolerance for this. If he

now knew the value of love, he demanded all the more from love, not realising that love itself is subject to the conditions of growth, that it still struggles—upwards, it is true—but struggles. And he could not practise it in his own life. Because the people at Basil worshipped him for that which was worthless, he despised them ; because they cast contempt on his "real knowledge, the few truths gained at a life's cost," he hated them. He could see no good in, and no hope for, men who were so blind. And why ?

> " In my own heart love had not been made wise
> To trace love's faint beginnings in mankind,
> To know even hate is but a mask of love's,
> To see a good in evil, and a hope
> In ill-success ; to sympathise, be proud
> Of their half-reasons, faint aspirings, dim
> Struggles for truth, their poorest fallacies,
> Their prejudice and fears and cares and doubts ;
> All with a touch of nobleness, despite
> Their error, upward tending all though weak,
> Like plants in mines which never saw the sun,
> But dream of him and guess where he may be,
> And do their best to climb and get to him."

But now, dying, he whom the sun's radiance had dazzled knew, that for those who have never seen the sun, yet the same sun shines ;

it is to them and to him the same source of
life, one and eternal. It all came back to the
same thing ;—life is one, and he who neglects
the weakest manifestation of life in others
neglects a gift of God to himself :—

> " Not so, dear child
> Of after-days, wilt thou reject the past
> Big with deep warnings of *the proper tenure*
> *By which thou hast the earth :* for thee the present
> Shall have distinct and trembling beauty, seen
> Beside that past's own shade when, in relief,
> Its brightness shall stand out : nor yet on thee
> Shall burst the future, as successive zones
> Of several wonder open on some spirit
> Flying secure and glad from heaven to heaven :
> But thou shalt painfully attain to joy,
> While hope and fear and love shall keep thee man ! "

It was just this, the secret of the proper tenure
by which the earth is held, that he had spent
a lifetime in learning. It was, after all, a com-
prehensive lesson, nothing less than the meaning of life, the meaning of death, the meaning
of life's limitations, and of death's possibilities. Truly a lifetime were well spent in
learning it. Happy he who, like Paracelsus,
masters it before he dies, and can "go joyous
back to God." For Paracelsus now knows
that the unquenchable thirst which has urged

him on from youth up till now was given
him to be satisfied. God was pledged to fill
the creature full whom he had made thus
hungry. It was in forsaking the "instincts
of that happy time," when "God was pledged
to take him by the hand," so long as the hand
was held out, that he had lost courage and
hope. Now in the pardon of Aprile he sees
the earnest of his own pardon :—

> "——If they have filled him full
> With magical music, as they freight a star
> With light, and have remitted all his sin,
> They will forgive me too; I too shall know!"

This blessed pardon, carrying with it, as it
does, the completion of the nature of each,
leads up to a higher note still, the note of
the old indomitable faith of his boyhood :—

> "And this is Death! . . .
> . . . . If I stoop
> Into a dark tremendous sea of cloud,
> It is but for a time; I press God's lamp
> Close to my breast; its splendour, soon or late,
> Will pierce the gloom: I shall emerge one day."

Thus "after last returns the first." The same
note is struck here as when he went out once
before into a region similarly trackless, only

seeing his way "as birds their trackless way,"
only confident of arriving because "He guides
me and the bird." He is now confident of
emerging one day, only because the unquenchable lamp of God must pierce any gloom,
however dense. He

> "——throws himself on God, and unperplexed
>   Seeking shall find him."

CAPONSACCHI.

"O soldier-saint !"

THE beginning of *The Ring and the Book*
repels us. It is not so much that we en-
dorse Carlyle's characteristic comment,—"What
a fuss about an Old Bailey trial!" but that
it is a miserable story. Not even the touching
picture of Pompilia as she was before the
supreme revelation came to her, her beauty
and transcendent purity of soul, can counteract
the shudder with which we read of Guido,
"half wolf, half man;" of his mother, the
"unmotherly mother, and unwomanly woman;"
of his brothers, rapacious and pitiless; of the
Comparini, the "ambiguous creatures," too
weak to be distinctly good or bad, yet strong
enough, the woman at least, to hoodwink and
to plot, to lie and to deceive,—

"Two poor ignoble hearts, who did their best,
Part God's way, part the other way than God's,
To somehow make a shift and scramble through
The world's mud."

Everywhere we find the same struggling towards selfish ends ; greed, lust, cruelty ; every
where the law of expediency reigning and
devotion to " the shows of things."

In the midst of all this murk and gloom, this
tangled web of low motives and ambitions,
suddenly there is

> " The cleaving of a cloud, a cry, a crash,
>   .   .   . cower'd i' the dust the crew,
>   As, in a glory of armour like St. George,"

Caponsacchi appears in the arena, with

> " Great, undisguised leap over post and pale,
>   Right into the mid-cirque, free fighting-place,"

Caponsacchi, the man with the upward glance
and the heart of gold, with "the broad brow
that reverberates the truth, and flashed the
word God gave him back to man," with the
" purity of soul that *will not* take pollution,"
which neither "the contagion of the world's
slow stain," nor the fiery pang of a sudden,
sharp temptation has any power to taint. He
now takes up the task shirked by those whose
special duty it was, and with a steadfast gaze
upon the eternal truth of things, ignoring
danger and almost certain misrepresentation,
he leaves the straight and safe path, and suc-
cours the oppressed. From this time forward

we breathe a new atmosphere; a light not seen before shines upon the scene.

And yet the character of Caponsacchi, man and priest, is not a simple one. There are some souls that are pure as snow; some that are pure as fire. Caponsacchi's was the latter. Although, equally with Pompilia, he tends upward, his was not the purity that no taint can come near, but rather the purity that is kept intact in the heart of it, saved, yet "so as by fire," the fire which burns and agonizes, and out of the throes leaves the pure gold. He had lived in the world "a man of the age and priest beside," "young, bold, handsome,"

> "Popular in the city, far and wide
> Famed, since Arezzo's but a little place,
> As the best of good companions, grave and gay
> At the decent minute; settled in his stall,
> Or sidling, lute on lap, by lady's couch,
> Ever the courtly Canon,"

with "wit at will, tact at every pore." His innate honesty of soul had caused him to pause, awe-struck, before taking the final vow to renounce the world :—

> "How shall holiest flesh
> Engage to keep such vow inviolate?
> How much less mine? I know myself too weak,
> Unworthy! Choose a worthier, stronger man!"

Although surrounded by others whose lives
were inconsistent with their vows, he shrank
from the hollowness of it. But reassured by
his superiors that, even if he should still play
the "fribble and coxcomb," yet he should, as
priest, "nowise break word," he finally became
a priest, and entered upon a life in which

> "—— mingling each its multifarious wires,
> Now heaven, now earth, now heaven and earth at once,
> Had plucked at and perplexed their puppet here ; "

a life in which the lust of the eye, "earthly
praise, repute o' the world, the flourish of loud
trump, the softer social fluting," enticed him
on every side, while the ideals of his order
pointed him to the rugged mountain path.
Satisfied, however, that he could live thus and
still hold his head erect, he conformed
himself :—

> "I . . . . both read the breviary
> And wrote the rhymes, was punctual in my place
> I' the Pieve, and as diligent at my post
> Where beauty and fashion rule."

And all the time there was the entirely serious
side of the man in the background, a great
reserve of strength, passion and enthusiasm.
His meeting with Pompilia did indeed supply

the spark which drew fire from him ; but it
could not have created the " whole store of
strengths eating into his heart which craved
employ," which he becomes so keenly conscious of at this point, although it supplied the
vent for their activity. Frivolous as his life
had seemed on the outside, he had thought
deeply :—

"I have thought sometimes, and thought long and hard,"

he tells his judges ;

> " I have stood before, gone round a serious thing,
> Tasked my whole mind to touch and clasp it close,
> As I stretch forth my arm to touch this bar.
> God and man, and what duty I owe both,—
> I dare to say I have confronted these
> In thought."

To such a man as this, with a vast reserve
of unexerted powers, clamorous to find vent,
the first genuine call for help was as powerful
as the cry of distressed maiden to the Red-
Cross Knight. Caponsacchi, before and after
his meeting with Pompilia, seems to have
been two different men ; and there was a very
distinct difference so far that the "revelation
of Pompilia," with which he tells us he was
"blessed," was at once the lightning-flash which

revealed the man to himself and the power which brought into action all the latent forces of his nature. But the man who saved Pompilia must always have been true and pure, nor does any man acquire a great fund of strength and self-forgetfulness suddenly, under the influence of a strong emotion. During his fribble and coxcomb days these qualities of heart and mind must have existed, and have been developing in Caponsacchi, as

> " The strawberry grows underneath the nettle ;
> And wholesome berries thrive and ripen best,
> Neighbour'd by fruit of baser quality."

Harry of England did not turn sage in a day, no matter what the history books say ; Shakespeare knew best.

Nevertheless, the meeting with Pompilia was the great crisis in the life of Caponsacchi, the turning point. It began that day in the theatre when he

> "—— saw enter, stand, and seat herself
> A lady, young, tall, beautiful, strange and sad,"

And she chanced to look at him.

> " That night and next day did the gaze endure,
> Burnt to my brain, as sunbeam thro' shut eyes,
> And not once changed the beautiful sad strange smile."

Ere the week was out an unwonted discontent
with the whole course of his life filled him.
What was the use and the end of it all?

> "'Tis but poor work this—
> Counting one's fingers till the sonnet's crowned.
> . . . . . Luckily Lent is near;
> Who cares to look will find me in my stall
> At the Pieve, constant to this faith at least—
> Never to write a canzonet any more!"

The first action of his awakened powers
shows itself in the effort to be more of
the priest, less of the worldling. His first
impulse is to continue in the wonted rut,
only henceforth in earnest. His devotion to
his stall in church attracts the notice of his
patron. "Are you turning Molinist?" the
latter asks. "Sir, what if I turned Christian?"
is the answer. Thus does he try to mend his
life in the way that lay nearest to him. But
the truth was gradually borne in upon him
that his life was shaken to its lowest depths,—

> "———broke short indeed,
> And showed the gap 'twixt what is, what should be."

He had arrived at the point which many
people—not all—reach at least once in their
lives, when they find themselves at a "crag's
sheer edge." They have come to an abrupt

halt, when life seems cut in two; when there
is no going back, and no going on without
a descent into the abyss. Such at least did
Caponsacchi's life seem to him on that night
when Pompilia at last

> "——took to the open, stood and stared
> With her wan white face to see where God might wait—
> And found there—Caponsacchi."

Now, when the distinct cry for help comes,
the spark is applied to all those blind struggling
powers within him, only half understood by
himself. Now for the first time the real man
shows himself. The change is overwhelming.
All that night he paces the city, impotent to
stem the tide which sweeps over his soul:

> "In rushed new things, the old were rapt away;
>   Alike abolished—the imprisonment
>   Of the outside air, the inside weight o' the world
>   That pulled me down.   .   .   .   .
>   .   .   .   .
>   Into another state, under new rule
>   I knew myself was passing swift and sure;
>   Whereof the initiatory pang approached;
>   I
>   Lay and let come the proper throe would thrill
>   Into the ecstasy and out-throb pain."

But the grey of the dawn finds him again
before the Church; and this time again, only

more strongly than before, does his quickened insight, the extension of his horizon, incline him towards obedience to his order, in spite of the revolution which has shaken his soul, or rather in virtue of it ; for he now sees in a new light his relationship to the Church, which has taken his plighted troth; and never again for him can there be any trifling with anything whatever. Now that he realises in himself for the first time that

> " ——life and death
> Are means to an end, that passion uses both,
> Indisputably mistress of the man
> Whose form of worship is self-sacrifice,"

he now knows first the duty of obedience. For "the revelation of Pompilia" was not personal, partial. It led him into *all* truth, or it was not true at all. There could be no such thing as a conflict between his duty to God and his duty to her. Duty to God was duty to her. This explains why, at this meeting with her, he says to her, "I am yours;" and he goes home and decides to leave her. Strange, one may say. But it was natural, fitting. Hear his own interpretation of it :—

> "Sirs, I obeyed. Obedience was too strange,—
> This new thing that had been struck into me

By the look o' the lady,—to dare disobey
The first authoritative word.   'T was God's.
I had been lifted to the level of her,
Could take such sounds into my sense.   I said
' We too are cognisant o' the master now ;
' She it is bids me bow the head : how true,
' I am priest !   I see the function here ;
' I thought the other way self-sacrifice :
' This is the true, seals up the perfect sum.
' I pay it, sit down, silently obey.' "

Two days later he sees Pompilia again ; and
this time a lightning-flash reveals to him a
higher law than that of his order.   A resolve to
save Pompilia at any price takes possession of
him without a struggle.   He neither hesitates
nor questions.   The suddenness of the light and
the reality of the consequent conviction is such
that Caponsacchi himself, in telling of this,
never thinks of commenting upon it.   She
makes known to him once more the extremity
of her need, and the answer comes prompt and
decisive :—

" Lady, waste no thought, no word
Even to forgive me !   Care for what I care—
Only !   Now follow me as I were fate !
Leave this house in the dark to-morrow night,
Just before daybreak :—there's new moon this eve—
It sets, and then begins the solid black.
Descend, proceed to the Torrione, step
Over the low dilapidated wall,

> Take San Clemente, there's no other gate
> Unguarded at the hour ; some paces thence
> An inn stands ; cross to it ; I shall be there."

Thus is the die cast ; and we too who read, in spite of Caponsacchi's former resolution, accept his action as the expected, the inevitable. And yet, although this is that point in the life of Caponsacchi which calls forth all that is highest and best in him, it is at the same time the point of extreme danger. For here he enters upon the abnormal, the exceptional ; he ventures upon a trackless sea without a chartered pilot. True he carried within him the pilot of the true heart and pure ; but what man can always order his own going ? And who can tell us when the duty of choice is laid upon us ? For the question where the duty of obedience ends and the duty of resistance begins has ever been one of the hardest to decide. How far ought a man to submit himself to rule, how far to follow his own impulses ? Loyalty, *esprit de corps*, the spirit of unity, unselfishness, all proclaim with a loud voice that a man ought to abide by his order. We can conceive of no fixed basis of human action, no great sustained effort, if we

K

once admit the principle that the individual instinct is to be the guide of each. " True guidance," Carlyle has said, "in return for loving obedience, did he but know it, is man's prime need." Caponsacchi was guide to himself. That he, a priest, should carry off from her husband Pompilia, a wife, was a distinct casting off of authority ; and in thus being a law to himself he did that which for the large majority of men would have been wrong. He had, it is true, arrived at a point where no true guidance other than his own conscience was to be had ; and his conscience spoke with no wavering voice. And if it was a wholly exceptional crisis he brought a wholly exceptional nature to bear upon it. This unerring instinct, gift of the strong-souled and the pure in heart, to the awe and wonder of their weaker brethren, who cannot live without rules and precedents, was one of Caponsacchi's leading characteristics. But he was doing that which could not be justified in principle, even though the action was justified ; he was making the individual instinct the guide. That it did not err in his case was owing to the nobility of the individual man. A less noble man might have had for the moment the same

generous impulse, and yet have been unable to
guide his steps upon the path that Caponsacchi
trod assured. No man that was not true, pure,
strong, single-eyed, self-sacrificing, intrepid,
could have gone on to the end without sin or
failure of one kind or another. Again, an
ignoble man might well have had an ignoble
instinct; and so have erred in following it.
As Innocent XII. puts it very trenchantly, if
Caponsacchi was right in following his impulse
to save Pompilia, then Guido was also right in
following his impulse to murder her. True, one
man's instinct may guide him aright, but,

> " Will he repeat the prodigy? Perhaps.
> Can he teach others how to quit themselves,
> Show why this step was right, while that were wrong?
> How should he? 'Ask your hearts as I asked mine.'"

And yet, our instinct is surely not playing us
false when it tells us that Caponsacchi was
right and not wrong at all. We know that
the chivalry

> " That dares the right and disregards alike
> The yea and nay of the world "

is wholly good. The strong rock of safety
in Caponsacchi's case was, the man was true
and single-eyed, and he was pure. His was

the "symmetric soul" which made him look
straight and go straight. In his whole action
he had no double object. The light was upon
his path ; and he walked assured,

> " Learning anew the use of soldiership,
>   Self-abnegation, freedom from all fear,
>   Loyalty to the life's end."

After his first meeting with Pompilia, he tells
his judges,

> " The spark of truth was struck from out our souls—
>   .   .   .   .   the first glance told me
> There was no duty patent in the world
> Like daring to be good and true myself,
> Leaving the shows of things to the Lord of Show,
> And Prince o' the power of the Air."

And he was pure :

> " In thought, word, and deed,
> How throughout all thy warfare thou wast pure,
> I find it easy to believe,"

is the testimony of the Pope. This Pompilia
felt instinctively without a question, when first
brought face to face with him, in spite of
overwhelming evidence to the contrary.   Her
first words are,—

> " Friend, foolish words were borne from you to me ;
> Your soul behind them is the pure strong wind."

She neither hesitates nor questions ; she knows.
" As I," he tells us,

> " Recognised her at potency of truth,
>   So she, by the crystalline soul, knew me,
>   Never mistook the signs."

It is the power of this invincible truth and
purity of soul which places both not alone
beyond the reach of evil, but even beyond the
reach of danger.   For

> "———See !
> Pompilia wife, and Caponsacchi priest,
> Are brought together as nor priest nor wife
> Should stand, and there is passion in the place,
> Power in the air for evil as for good,
> Promptings from heaven and hell, as if the stars
> Fought in their courses for a fate to be.
> Thus stand the wife and priest, a spectacle,
> I doubt not, to unseen assemblage there.
> No lamp will mark that window for a shrine,
> No tablet signalise the terrace, teach
> New generations which succeed the old
> The pavement of the street is holy ground ;
> No bard describe in verse how Christ prevailed
> And Satan fell like lightning."

And, with Caponsacchi, it was the purity of
strength, not of ignorance or weakness. If he
disclaimed utterly the idea that either he or
Pompilia could have written " the vulgar and
impure banalities called letters about love," it

was because, as he tells his judges, he, " a
priest and loveless both," could teach them
what love really was. What Pompilia felt by
instinct, when, in her shrinking from her
husband, she cried, " His soul has never lain
beside my soul," Caponsacchi's keen eyes pene-
trated within and without. As he was a
complete human being, not a disembodied
spirit, he knew only too well that, since he
was condemned to live his life in the " old
solitary nothingness," while he could dream
of what life might be, " companioned by the
woman there," the highest faculty in him was
maimed, inarticulate, that he missed the very
fulness of life here on earth, that sacramental
mystery in which things unseen express themselves in things seen ; but,—and this again
because he was a complete man, not one in
whom the human endowment of a God-allied
spirit is left out or crushed out of life,—that
the outward expression without the eternal
reality behind was a false thing. What
Pompilia was to him he did not ignore, nor
was he careful to conceal :

> "—— I apprise you—in contempt
> For all misapprehending ignorance

O' the human heart, much more the mind of Christ,—
That I assuredly did bow, was blessed
By the revelation of Pompilia. There !
Such is the final fact I fling you, Sirs,"

he tells his judges ; but whatever his feeling
for her was, it could not exist, given the
circumstances of both, with what went by the
name of love in the trial, where the word
was bandied about among things untrue and
unworthy,—that false, unlovely thing which
comes to us clothed as an angel of light, but
inwardly " maketh a lie." No temptation even
seems to have come to him in the presence of
Pompilia ; we cannot find a trace of any
vulgar struggle with himself during all that
long journey to Rome. How could there be
such ? He was stirred to his inmost depths,
perplexed, over-awed ; but he was uplifted to
a region into which no unworthy thought can
enter. The influence of Pompilia had ever
been the same over him :

" You know this is not love, Sirs,—it is faith,
The feeling that there's God, He reigns and rules
Out of this low world."

Joined to all this was the reverence of the

strong for the weak of the essentially manly
man.   He possessed the sense

> "That reads, as only such can read, the mark
>   God sets on woman, signifying so
>   She should—shall peradventure—be divine;
>   Yet 'ware, the while, how weakness mars the print
>   And makes confusion, leaves the thing men see,
>   —Not this man sees,—who from his soul re-writes
>   The obliterated charter,—love and strength
>   Mending what's marred."

This tender chivalry in himself is hidden from
Caponsacchi, for what does he say?

> "———— For Pompilia be advised,
>   Build churches, go pray! You will find me there."

Thus while to her he seems to stoop, to himself he ever seems to look up.

And the final catastrophe, the murder of
Pompilia and his subsequent examination, call
into action another side of the man, hitherto
dormant.   He whose tenderness aroused such
wonder in Pompilia that she asked him what
woman he had been used to serve so gently,
is uncontrolled in his anger, scathing in his
scorn, when he finds himself before the men
through whose supineness the crime has been
made possible.

" . . . . . . There stands he,
. . . .
There, where you yesterday heard Guido speak,
Speaks Caponsacchi . . . . .
Here sit the old Judges then, but with no grace
Of reverend carriage, magisterial port :
For why? The accused of eight months since
. . . .
Now is grown judge himself, terrifies now
This, now the other culprit called a judge,
Whose turn it is to stammer and look strange,
As he speaks rapidly, angrily, speech that smites :
And they keep silence, bear blow after blow,
Because the seeming solitary man,
Speaking for God, may have an audience too,
Invincible, no discreet Judge provokes."

The words of Caponsacchi do in truth bear fire
enough to burn away like chaff all vain de-
fences, all false superstructures that can hide
the truth from the light of day :—

"Answer you, Sirs? Do I understand aright?
Have patience ! In this sudden smoke from hell,—
So things disguise themselves,—I cannot see
My own hand held thus broad before my face
And know it again."   .   .   .   .
 .   .   .   .
 .   .   .   .   .   "If any of you
Dares think that I, i' the face of death, her death
That's in my eyes and ears and brain and heart,
Lie,—if he does, let him ! I mean to say,
So he stop there, stay thought from smirching her,
The snow-white soul that angels fear to take

Untenderly. But, all the same, I know
I, too, am taintless, and I bare my breast.
You can't think, men as you are, all of you,
But that, to hear thus suddenly such an end
Of such a wonderful white soul, that comes
Of a man and murderer calling the white black,
Must shake me, trouble and disadvantage. Sirs,
Only seventeen ! "   .   .   .   .   .   .

.   .   .   .
.   .   .   .   " Men,
You must know that a man gets drunk with truth
Stagnant inside him ! Oh, they've killed her, Sirs !
Can I be calm ? "

But it is in his last words that the whole
man, living and breathing, in his strength and
weakness, aspiring, struggling, attaining, loving,
and lovable, shows himself more fully :—

"You see we are
So very pitiable, she and I,
Who had conceivably been otherwise.
Forget distemperature and idle heat !
Apart from truth's sake, what's to move so much ?
Pompilia will be presently with God ;
I am, on earth, as good as out of it,
A relegated priest ; when exile ends
I mean to do my duty and live long.
She and I are mere strangers now ; but priests
Should study passion ; how else cure mankind,
Who come for help in passionate extremes ?
I do but play with an imagined life
Of who, unfettered by a vow, unblessed
By the higher call,—since you will have it so,—

> Leads it companioned by the woman there
> To live, and see her learn, and learn by her,
> Out of the low obscure and petty world—
> Or only to see one purpose and one will
> Evolve themselves i' the world, change wrong to right:
> To have to do with nothing but the true,
> The good, the eternal—and these, not alone
> In the main current of the general life,
> But small experiences of every day,
> Concerns of the particular hearth and home:
> To learn not only by a comet's rush
> But a rose's birth,—not by the grandeur, God—
> But the comfort, Christ. All this, how far away!"

Far away!—and yet through all the sadness there is the note of triumph. If the words are spoken from the standpoint of the exile at the gate, the woman whom he saved and crowned knew him best, and she it is who tells us,

> "Through such souls alone
> God stooping shows sufficient of His light
> For us i' the dark to rise by."

TWO POEMS ON PAINTERS
AND THEIR ART.

THE reader of Browning's poetry cannot fail to be struck by the large number of poems which are devoted to artists and their art, as well as by the countless allusions to art prodigally scattered throughout, all showing how strongly he was attracted to the subject. It has sometimes been said that he seems to cast discredit upon art, as in one well-known passage in *The Last Ride Together* :—

> "And you, great sculptor—so, you gave
> A score of years to art, her slave,
> And that's your Venus, whence we turn
> To yonder girl that fords the burn !
> You acquiesce————"

But this certainly does not reflect Browning's own attitude. In a dramatic monologue one may believe that, when he represents a lover consoling himself for a lost mistress by calling

up the failures of other men, artists included,
he is not of necessity giving utterance to his
own deliberate conclusions on art.   It is not
a very profound reflection at the best; for the
comparison is between two things which do
not compare,—the marble Venus and the little
mountain maid having two very different parts
to play in life, the worth of neither detracting
from that of the other.   An entirely opposite
view, and one which we cannot but feel is
more in accordance with Browning's own, is
expressed in *Fra Lippo Lippi*:—

> "We're made so that we love
> First when we see them painted things we've passed
> Perhaps a hundred times, nor cared to see;
> And so they're better painted—better to us,
> Which is the same thing.   Art was given for that;
> God uses us to help each other so,
> Lending our minds out."

It is true that Browning was always a man
first, an artist next; and even in those poems
in which the central figure is an artist, it will
generally be found that the broadly human
interest is paramount; as in *Andrea del Sarto*,
for instance, where our main concern throughout is with the man as a man.   Further we
find that, even when he deals directly with

art itself, his views on the subject are largely bound up with his view of life as a whole; and with him art is always subordinated to life. This is brought out in a passage in *James Lee's Wife*, which, while seeming, read superficially, to depreciate art, only assigns to art what Browning conceives to be its proper place as the interpreter of life, of that which is greater than itself. Thus that "Art for Art's sake" never was, never could have been, an article of his creed, is abundantly evident; but this was due to the fact that his larger enthusiasm for human life as a whole towered so high above his interest in and feeling for any special side of human life; not that he was not fully alive to the value of art.

There is, however, a manifest crudity in the extension of any such distinction; since art, looked at in its length and breadth, may almost be said to be an essential condition of life—as essential as worship, and almost co-extensive with it, co-extensive certainly with any effort to bridge over the gulf between the seen and the unseen. Even the savage, when he approaches his god, seizes upon art as the only means of expressing him; and the language of his every-day intercourse falls into a rude lilt. But there must be much confusion of thought, as well as much difficulty in expressing one's thought, so long as we are without a generally accepted definition of art. Tolstoi, in his *What is Art?* has given us fifty-seven definitions of art from the pens of artists, poets, philosophers, psychologists, scientists, novelists, statesmen, — French, German, Italian, Dutch, and English, a goodly company. And then he tells us that they are all wrong! He next goes on to give us another of his own. That makes fifty-eight. All this is very confusing; one feels that one may as well give up all hope of ever arriving at a definition that will satisfy every one. One broad distinction, however, in the views of those who write about art comes to the front at once;—some give to it a distinctly ethical function, some do not; and Browning belongs to the former class. According to his view, art does not indeed exist for utility; for art is

> " the love of loving, rage
> Of knowing, seeing, feeling the absolute truth of things
> For truth's sake, whole and sole, not any good truth brings
> The knower, seer, feeler, beside."

But, although truth may be sought quite apart
from gain, the knowledge of truth must bring
gain all the same ; and art with Browning has
just this function,—it shows " the absolute
truth of things " to those who could not see
it without its aid.   For, as he tells us elsewhere, the artist is he who has—

> " Head—to look up not downward, hand—of power
> To make head's gain the portion of a world
> Where else the uninstructed ones too sure
> Would take all outward beauty—film that's furled
> About a star—for the star's self, endure
> No guidance to the central glory,—nay,
> (Sadder) might apprehend the film was fog,
> Or (worst) wish all but vapour well away,
> And sky's pure product thickened from earth's bog."

The whole story of Aprile illustrates this,—
Aprile, who, because he has neglected to use
his gift for the benefit of his fellow-men, is
represented as a " recreant to his race,"—one
who has betrayed a sacred trust, since he has
" left the world, he was to loosen, bound."
Art is to be to the artist a means of growth,
to the world a means of enlightenment ; thus
it " blesses him that gives and him that
takes."

Browning was strongly drawn to art in all

its forms, and to artists of all classes ; but he seems to have found the most attractive personalities in the ranks of painters ; •and he has written more about them than about artists of any other kind. The poems in which he deals directly with painters and their art stand before us in goodly profusion ; and although not written by Browning with any such design, they illustrate in a kind of sequence different phases in the history of art :—Greek art, early mediæval art (*Old Pictures in Florence*), later mediæval art, early Renaissance art (*Fra Lippo Lippi*), later Renaissance art (*The Bishop orders his Tomb at St. Praxed's, Andrea del Sarto*) ; while his own views on art bring us down to the Pre-Raphaelite movement of our own day.

Of these poems, two in particular illustrate admirably two tendencies against which art has always had to struggle,—against which it is inevitable that art must always have to struggle ;—the tendency on the one hand to ignore things unseen, on the other to depreciate things seen. For art must have both sides,—the real (the concrete) and the mystical. The Pre-Raphaelites promul-

L

gated no new doctrine when they demanded
of art "uncompromising truth to nature in the
rendering of visible things" joined to "a vivid
realisation of things unseen." The true artist
in all ages combines these two. Art, which has
for its object the interpretation of things seen
so that the unseen is revealed by and *in* them,
cannot depreciate the one or the other without
loss. But, since art lies in two regions which,
to a sense, not finely poised, of the true relationships of things, seem so wide apart, it is inevitable
that, among the rank and file of those who follow
art, there will often arise an undue emphasising
of the one side to the neglect of the other; and
this very often takes the form of a tendency to
separate the simple, the homely, and the familiar
from the mystical and the awe-inspiring. The
true artist makes no such divorce. He who
approaches all things in a "temper of wonder,
reverence, and awe," to him all things are
wonderful; but it has happened in the history
of art that tendencies towards such a divorce
have arisen—tendencies against which the
greatest have always endeavoured to struggle.

The Italian painters of the thirteenth century
aimed at representing the invisible through their

art. They themselves made no mistake about it ; they knew that this was best accomplished by fidelity to nature ; but later, their successors, in their striving after the invisible, arrived in time at a method by which they represented the visible in a manner in which all fidelity to nature was forgotten or despised as unnecessary. Thereupon arose the art of the Renaissance with its exuberant sensuousness, its insistence upon the value of mere physical life. And in any movement of reform on the one side or on the other, the swinging of the pendulum just a little too far has always to be calculated upon. All this, and much more, is strikingly brought out in two poems of Browning's, *Old Pictures in Florence* and *Fra Lippo Lippi ;* the watch-word of the one being, "Bring the invisible full into play ;" of the other, "The value and significance of flesh."

Old Pictures in Florence was written in 1845, at a time when ideas of a revolution in art must have been surging in the brain of Rossetti, and three years before the formation of the Pre-Raphaelite Brotherhood. In this poem Browning, if he does not anticipate, at least shows himself in sympathy with one of the leading tendencies of the movement, in recognising the great work which the early mediæval artists did ; and protesting against the neglect into which their works have fallen. He goes back with tender regret to that " season of Art's spring-birth so dim and dewy," when Cimabue and Giotto endeavoured, by patient and faithful study of nature, to create a new art, which would take the place of the art which they saw all around them, and which had long since proved itself incapable of answering to the needs of men,—a veritable renaissance in itself.

The poet, by a gift which, he tells us, God grants him now and then, looking upon Florence, sees, not alone her living men and women, " who chirp and chaffer, come and go for pleasure or profit," but also the spirits of the ancient masters, whose works lie neglected and dishonoured and falling into decay. If one searches for them in chapter-house or cloister-porch, in the church's apse, aisle, or nave, sometimes even in the dark crypt where one has to grope one's way by the light of a torch, everywhere there is the same neglect. The frescoes peel and drop, and no hand is held out

to arrest the decay ; and all the time the shades
of the wronged great souls look on in silence.
To the common herd they are " Old Master
This and Early the Other"; only the faithful few
know that the old and the new are fellows and
that these early painters, many of them unnamed
and forgotten, did a work without which there
would have been no Da Vinci, no Angelo, no
Raphael :

"For oh, this world and the wrong it does !
  They are safe in heaven with their backs to it,
The Michaels and Rafaels, you hum and buzz
  Round the works of, you of little wit !
Do their eyes contract to the old world's scope,
  Now that they see God face to face,
And have all attained to be poets, I hope ?
  'Tis their holiday now, in any case."

Much they reck of your praise and you !
  But the wronged great souls—can they be quit
Of a world where their work is all to do,
  .   .   .   . "

They linger round, not for the praise missed,
but for the work undone.   They had a
message for the world ; and can they rest
until the world has heard it ?

Their message was shortly this.   " Greek Art
ran and reached the goal."   The Greeks depicted

the human form, body and soul united, in flaw-
less perfection. So much was clear gain ;—

> " The truth of Man, as by God first spoken,
>   Which the actual generations garble,
>   Was re-uttered————"

But their art failed in that it took no account
of the infinite. Its very perfection was the
seal of its incompleteness, looked at in the light
of absolute truth and beauty. It was perfect,
therefore " the Artificer's hand was arrested ; "
the avenues to further progress were closed.
And all the time, lying above and beyond it,
was that vast region of the unseen, which it
could not touch. There was no mystery
about this art. Perfection of outward form
was something tangible, which the eye could '
estimate, the senses apprehend. The better
thing beyond, which no eye can see, was only
to be indicated by an art which would reach
out through and above itself towards that which
it could never hope adequately to represent.
Thus Greek art led to nothing ; men, looking
upon this perfection, were paralysed :—

> " So, you saw yourself as you wished you were,
>   As you might have been, as you cannot be ;
>   Earth here, rebuked by Olympus there ;
>   And grew content with your poor degree,

With your little power, by those statues' godhead,
  And your little scope, by their eyes' full sway,
And your little grace, by their grace embodied,
  And your little date, by their forms that stay.

.   .   .   .

So, testing your weakness by their strength,
  Your meagre charms by their rounded beauty,
Measured by Art in your breadth and length,
  You learned—to submit is a mortal's duty."

This was all that that period of Greek art could do for men,—show them perfection, make them feel how weak and imperfect they were, and how vain it was to aim at that which they could never attain to.

The change came when some one "turned his eyes inwardly one fine day, and cried with a start—'What if we so small be greater and grander the while than they?'" It was then that the early masters began to paint. They aimed at something far beyond the goal of Greek art, so far beyond that they never hoped to show it in its perfection; but they did accomplish this,—they brought "the invisible full into play;" at the same time that they painted, or aimed at painting, man as he was, not as he might have been. Their art was imperfect; but its very imperfection hinted at something beyond, and growth again became possible. "To-day's brief passion seethes with the morrow" they could cry—

> " 'Tis a lifelong toil till our lump be leaven—
> The better ! What's come to perfection perishes.
> Things learned on earth we shall practice in heaven ;
> Works done least rapidly, Art most cherishes."

And men, looking at their pictures, could see themselves as they were, no better, and yet with infinite possibilities suggested.

> " On which I conclude, that the early painters,
>   To cries of 'Greek Art and what more wish you ?'—
> Replied, 'To become now self-acquainters,
>   'And paint man, whatever the issue !
> 'Make new hopes shine through the flesh they fray,
>   'New fears aggrandize the rags and tatters :
> 'To bring the invisible full into play !
>   'Let the visible go to the dogs—what matters ?' "

We cannot but feel that Browning's own view of the function of art in this respect largely coincides with that which he ascribes to the old masters, a view closely bound up with his philosophy of life as a whole. Art was to aim at that which it could not hope fully to accomplish. The higher the art, the more this held good, for the truer the truth that art was to interpret, the less was it possible to represent it in the concrete, and so it teaches as much by that which it leaves undone as by that which it does, always provided that it recognises and suggests the undone. An artist ought to choose rather to give inadequate expression to his highest conceptions than to represent in its perfection a lower conception. This is the view of art, with its corresponding view of life, to which Browning constantly recurs.

> "——See thou applaud the great heart of the artist,
>   Who, examining the capabilities
>   Of the block of marble he has to fashion
>   Into a type of thought or passion,—
>   Not always, using obvious facilities,
>   Shapes it, as any artist can,
>   Into a perfect symmetrical man,
>   Complete from head to foot of the life-size,
>   Such as old Adam stood in his wife's eyes,—
>   But, now and then, bravely aspires to consummate
>   A Colossus by no means so easy to come at,
>   And uses the whole of his block for the bust,
>   Leaving the mind of the public to finish it,
>   Since cut it ruefully short he must :
>   On the face alone he expends his devotion,
>   He rather would mar than resolve to diminish it,
>   —Saying, ' Applaud me for this grand notion
>   ' Of what a face may be ! As for completing it
>   ' In breast and body and limbs, do that, you !' "

This was the value of the mass of marble

bought by the speaker in *Fifine at the Fair*
"for just ten dollars." To the world it was
an "uncouth, unwieldy bulk," shapeless and
meaningless; but to him it out-valued his
Raphael as the diamond the pearl; for "one
hand—the master's—smoothed and scraped that
bulk," and to the seeing eye it gave subtle
hints of what Michael Angelo's design had
been,—"the creature, dear-divine, yet earthly
—awful, too," the sea-goddess Eidothée. He,
the man who possessed it, worked out in his
soul of souls the whole design :—

> " For, you must know, I too achieved Eidothée
> In silence and by night—dared justify the lines
> Plain to my soul   .   .   .   .   .
> If she stood forth at last, the Master was to thank !
> Yet may there not have smiled approval in his eyes—
> That one at least was left who, born to recognise
> Perfection in the piece imperfect, worked that night,
> In silence, such his faith, until the apposite
> Design was out of him, truth palpable once more?
> And then,—for at one blow its fragments strewed the floor,—
> Recalled the same to live within his soul as heretofore."

In a strain half pathetic, half whimsical,
Browning now goes on to reproach the Old
Masters for numbering him among the un-
thinking crowd, who are too blind to recognise the value of their art; for would he not

willingly rescue their works from neglect, if
they would only give him a hint where anything but frescoes was to be found. Not that
he expects the greatest of them to deign to
accept his homage. The great Ghirlandajo,
Botticelli, Lippino, Frà Angelico, — he does
not aspire to be recognised by these ;—

> "But are you too fine, Taddeo Gaddi,
>   To grant me a taste of your intonaco,
> Some Jerome that seeks the heaven with a sad eye,
>   Not a churlish saint, Lorenzo Monaco ? "

Above all Giotto comes in for his share of the
reproaches ; since he, at least, ought to have
recognised Browning's long devotion. He can
bear the slights of the others, but Giotto !

> "Giotto, how, with that soul of yours,
>   Could you play me false who loved you so ? "

Had he not searched everywhere for one
piece of work of his in particular,—"a certain
precious little tablet Buonarroti eyed like a
lover ; " and in the end some one else un-
earthed it ? Why had not the ghost of Giotto
spoken to him in time, and given him a hint ?

He breaks off in a spirit prophetic and yet
not prophetic, with an aspiration after a time

when, the Grand Duke having been driven from Florence, Florence shall be a republic once more.   Then Florentines may

> "—— ponder, once Freedom restored to Florence,
> How art may return that departed with her."

Fra Lippo Lippi shows mediæval art in conflict with the growing spirit of the Renaissance.   From insisting on the importance of representing spirit rather than matter, the later mediæval artists went on to neglect the body.   This was the artistic milieu in which the painter-monk, Fra Lippino, found himself:

> "Your business is not to catch man with show,
> With homage to the perishable clay,
> But lift them over it, ignore it all,
> Make them forget there's such a thing as flesh.
> Your business is to paint the souls of men—
> .   .   .   .
> Give us no more of body than shows soul!
> Why put all thought of praise out of our head
> With wonder at lines, colours, and what not?
> Paint the soul, never mind the legs and arms!"

But it was not for nothing that Fra Lippo Lippi had spent eight years of his life in the streets.   He had learned the look of things; and he loved to paint men and women just as he saw them, not disembodied spirits.   Allowed to adorn his convent, he covers a cloister-wall

with a piece of surging life, in which monks
of all kinds and colours, old women, little
children, the murderer and the penitent, jostle
one another. The monks, good simple souls,
look and applaud.   This is art which appeals
to them. But the Prior and the men of the
old school look grave and shake their heads:—
" It's art's decline, my son," they say ; " you're
not of the true painters." He endeavours to
conform himself and paint as he is bidden ;
but he chafes against painting "saints and
saints and saints again," nothing more ; while
without a whole world of beauty and delight
lies under his eyes,—the world !

> " The beauty and the wonder and the power,
>   The shapes of things, their colours, lights and shades,
>   Changes, surprises,—and God made it all ! "

How can he look upon the fair face of his own
town of Florence, with

> "yonder river's line,
>   The mountain round it, and the sky above,
>   Much more the figures of man, woman, child,
>   These are the frame to,"

and say that all this is to be despised and
passed over ? No,

> "The world and life's too big to pass for a dream."

This was the idea that he wanted to show forth in his painting :—

> "———paint these
> Just as they are, careless what comes of it ;
> God's works—paint any one, and count it crime
> To let a truth slip."

And yet not altogether without idealising them ; for he knows that the artist is the interpreter, not the brainless repeater of a message in the same language in which it has been committed to him ; in particular when all can have the message in that language themselves first-hand. He knows that people understand things when painted, which they understand not at all when not painted. He will "lend his mind out" to help men to see that which they cannot see but for art ; he will interpret ; but he will interpret on no other principle than this,—

> "——— This world's no blot for us,
> Nor blank ; it means intensely, and means good."

And he insists upon this, that the same God who made the soul made the body also ; and that if the soul is to be revealed, it must be done in God's own way, by means of the body, not in spite of it. It was false art by which men painted the body badly, in order that the eye, unable to rest there, must go on to find the soul. Men are less, not more, tempted to " take the film that's furled about a star for the star's self," the more the central glory permeates the film. The more beautiful the external world, the more is the inner soul of things revealed.

This poem carries with it a breezy rush of life, a *Lebensfreudigkeit* which breathes the very spirit of the Renaissance. But it would be a mistake to suppose that, because Fra Lippo Lippi protests against what was undoubtedly the overstraining of one side of art to the neglect of the other, his art was merely sensuous, or that his theory of art was one-sided. He combats this in character-istic words :—

> " Why can't a painter lift each foot in turn,
> Left foot and right foot, go a double step,
> Make his flesh liker and his soul more like,
> Both in their order ? "

or if he does, for argument's sake,

> " ——say there's beauty with no soul at all
> (I never saw it—put the case the same—) "

his allowing of the case in no way affects his own attitude,—" I never saw it."

No true artist ever did. For he knows that all beauty is but the robe of truth, that truth which looms large, formless, awful, before his eyes. Herself he cannot see ; sometimes he only hears the rustle of the sweeping garment as she passes away beyond his sight ; but he treasures up each glimpse of her in sky and sea, in tree and stream, in the faces of men and women. In everything that his eye rests upon, he sees some outward manifestation of her ; and as he looks upon now one aspect, now another, now another, he seeks to embody the vision in forms that stay. Is his art perfect ? Surely not. For he knows that he will never see the whole with mortal eyes :—

> " I thirst for truth,
> But shall not drink it till I reach the source."

And how powerless is his brush to represent even that which he does see ! He must be satisfied if he can only show " some fragment, some slight sample of the prouder workmanship his own home boasts ; " if his art can thus " show its birth was in a gentler clime ; "

so that men, passing by, may reflect, before they depart, how splendid. must be the treasure-house from which these are taken.

And, like the scribe, who is " well instructed unto the kingdom of heaven," he " bringeth forth out of his treasure things new and old." He is not careful lest one aspect of the truth should seem to run counter to another. That is truth's affair ; his to see purely, and record faithfully. For the true artist there can be no possible opposition between the " real," so-called, and the " ideal ;" for he knows that both,—the thing seen and the thing unseen,—are one.

M

ANDREA DEL SARTO.

"'Friend, there's a certain sorry little scrub
'Goes up and down our Florence, none cares how,
'Who, were he set to plan and execute
'As you are, pricked on by your popes and kings,
'Would bring the sweat into that brow of yours!'"

So said Michael Angelo, "his very self," one
day to Raphael, while the latter was painting
the frescoes in the Vatican, "flaming out his
thoughts upon a palace wall for Rome to see,"
uplifted in soul. And the "sorry little scrub,"
who could rival, nay, out-rival the great master,
was Andrea del Sarto, called "the faultless
painter." Such, at least, is the popular story
which Browning rescues from neglect, and by
which he emphasises still further that which
he puts forward all through in his sketch, that
the failure of Andrea del Sarto to reach the
highest rank among painters was the failure of

one who could have attained, not that of one who was shut out by the limitations of his genius.

Andrea Vanucchi, commonly known as Andrea del Sarto (the tailor's Andrew), was born in Florence about the year 1488, and died in 1530, ten years after the death of Raphael. He drew his first inspirations from his studies of the pictures of Maraccio and Guirlandajo, of Leonardo and Michael Angelo ; and early showed conspicuous talent in draughts-manship, treatment of colour, light and shade, and all the technique of the art. He possessed an extraordinary facility for copying. We read that one copy that he made of a celebrated picture, Raphael's portrait of Leo X., deceived even the man who had painted most of the accessories, draperies, background, &c., himself. But his original pictures as well showed unusual power. Concerning one, a picture of the Last Supper, which he painted for the monastery of the Salvi, Lanzi tells the story of how " at the siege of Florence, in 1529, the soldiers, after having assailed the suburbs of the city, where the convent was situated, and destroyed the church and part of the monastery, on approaching the refectory, were so struck with the impressive beauty of this painting, that they remained motionless, and had not the heart to demolish it; imitating on that occasion the conduct of Demetrius, who, at the siege of Rhodes, respected only the paintings of Protogenes." The artist who could move men thus can hardly have been a mere clever draughtsman. Yet it is certain that his pictures fall far below the works of those painters of whom he seems by natural endowments to have been the peer. A biographer, writing in the beginning of the present century, gives us the following estimate of his art :—" His design is correct, and partakes of the style of M. Angelo; his compositions are agreeable, and his ordonnances are arranged with judgment. . . . His colouring is distinguished by the suavity and harmony of his tones; his pencil is full and flowing; and he has perhaps never been surpassed in the boldness of his relief, or his perfect knowledge of the chiar-oscuro ;" but the same writer adds, " He wanted that sacred fire which animates the great poet and the painter, and inspires them with their noblest and boldest conceptions." At the age of twenty-four he married Lucrezia

del Fede, a woman whose extreme beauty lives
to-day on many of his canvases, and who was
his evil genius all through life.   From this
time onwards there seems to have been a
struggle between two opposing forces in his
life,—his art which pointed him upwards, and
his wife who dragged him down ; and the
victory remained with her.   His golden
chance came when Francis I. called him to
his court; and there, in the warmth of the
great monarch's smile, it seemed as if he
could at last "leave the ground, put on the
glory ; " but he was called back to Florence
by his wife, and the avenues to further progress were closed for ever.   He left Fontaine-
bleau with the promise to return again, Francis
having entrusted him with money for the
purchase of works of art in Italy, which he
was to bring back with him.   But once again
in Florence, he forgot art, forgot honour, forgot even common honesty.   He appropriated
this money to his own use, and return to
France was now impossible.   From this time
onward he sank lower and lower, falling more
and more under the influence of his wife, and
painting only such pictures as would bring

in ready gain. He died while comparatively young, in extreme poverty, deserted by the woman for whom he had sacrificed art and life alike.

Andrea del Sarto had fallen on what were for him evil days. The great Renaissance was in full swing; the pioneers had done their work; and now it was for the rank and file to follow on into the breach, and along the path that they had opened out. Early as it was, signs were not wanting that pointed to that thraldom in which the great Raphael was to hold the world for three hundred years after his death. Signs of the method of Raphael becoming stereotyped into a set of dogmas, and of the evolution of a school after his manner, were springing up. And Andrea del Sarto, with his fatal facility of execution, found that he could paint pictures that pleased and sold, while working upon other men's lines, the " fundamental brain-work " absent.

But it was reserved for Browning to bring out the full pathos of all that this story implies; Browning, whose especial good gift it is to be able to breathe on the dry bones

of facts and make them live. He who, from
the bald records of an old murder case, could
evolve a Caponsacchi, a Pompilia, and an
Innocent XII., such as he presents him,
now breathes upon Vasari's biography, and
the man lives before us.

And it is an achievement peculiar to
Browning's self, that, in giving us this picture of a man without a moral backbone,
yet, so just is his estimate of him, so large
and generous his view of human nature at
its weakest, that the man is one to whom
our heart goes out in pity, not one from whom
we shrink back in contempt. And this in spite
of the fact that the moral failure is placed in
the most striking light, and that it is failure
which Browning's individual bent would cause
him to place in the category of sins of the
most deadly class; for is it not the deliberate
turning away from the light of a man to
whom light has been given, until at last the
moral nature is so weakened that a turning
back is impossible? But the man is generous,
gentle, and lovable. His love for Lucrezia is
not all passion of the lower kind; it is full
of tender making allowances, bearing with

excusing. Throughout it is the infinite pathos, the unutterable sadness of sin that oppresses us.

The picture is extraordinarily vivid. We see the man and the woman as they sit hand in hand in "the melancholy little house" they "built to be so gay with," built with the gold of the French King; we catch the twilight atmosphere of the whole; we feel the settled, hopeless melancholy of the man, a melancholy with which he has even ceased to struggle; all around seems to exhale a sigh in sympathy with that which goes up from his own soul :—

> " A common greyness silvers everything,—
> All in a twilight   .   .   .   .   .
> .   .   .   .
> My youth, my hope, my art, being all toned down,
> To yonder sober, pleasant Fiesole.
> There's the bell clinking from the chapel-top ;
> That length of convent-wall across the way
> Holds the trees safer, huddled more inside ;
> The last monk leaves the garden ; days decrease,
> And autumn grows, autumn in everything."

"My youth, my hope, my art," what volumes does this speak ! He is only thirty-seven years old; yet his life is practically over. All striving is over; he has failed, and he rests upon failure. And this is the painter whom men call faultless :—

> " I can do with my pencil what I know,
> What I see, what at bottom of my heart
> I wish for, if I ever wish so deep—
> Do easily too—when I say, perfectly,
> I do not boast, perhaps :   .   .   .
> I do what many dream of, all their lives,
> —Dream? strive to do, and agonise to do
> And fail in doing."

But his excelling is the seal of his failure ; for in conception, in effort, in true artistic fire, he has failed, failed with his eyes straight turned to the light. Is his work perfect ? but why ? Because he pitches his conception low ; because he "seeks a little thing to do, sees it and does it ;" chooses always a task well within his grasp. "Ah, but a man's reach should exceed his grasp." Did he but seek to express the highest conception that his inner soul of souls was capable of; had he, like Raphael, reached out, "that Heaven might so replenish him, above and through his art," then his execution, like Raphael's, would indeed have given way ; but "the play, the insight, the stretch" would have been all his. As it is, he, whose eye for form is so true that he can correct the faults in Raphael's work, never deceives himself as to his true place and rank. He knows that work perfect in the way that his is perfect means artistic failure ; nay, further, that artistic success such as his is means moral failure ; and that he falls far below, not alone Raphael and his compeers, but also many unnamed artists whose works have come to nothing, and who in actual achievement have done so much less than he :—

> " So much less !
> Well, less is more, Lucrezia, I am judged.
> There burns a truer light of God in them,
> In their vexed beating stuffed and stopped-up brain,
> Heart, or whate'er else, than goes to prompt
> This low-pulsed forthright craftsman's hand of mine.
> Their works drop groundward, but themselves, I know,
> Reach many a time a heaven that's shut to me,
> Enter and take their place there, sure enough,
> Though they come back and cannot tell the world.
> My works are nearer heaven, but I sit here."

Why is it ? Why, with so true an insight into what constitutes high work and low, does he conceive inferior work? For the extremity of the pathos is not in the artistic failure in itself, but in the lost possibilities. If he were merely a correct, soulless painter, there would be no cause for regret; but, as when we turn

from Millais' *Carpenter's Shop* or his *Isabella*
to his later work—his portraits of fashionable
ladies or over-dressed children,—here, too, we
can only exclaim with Othello, "But the pity
of it! oh, the pity of it!" And for Andrea
del Sarto the lowest, saddest depth of all is
touched in his acceptance of all this, his
resignation. He is satisfied; he no longer
even struggles. To the saddest, most hopeless
words of all—words that speak of final, unal-
terable failure in him to reach the place meant
for him by God, he adds, "As I choose."
Truly this is twilight, a twilight that carries
with it a promise of blackest midnight.

The main cause of all lies in this fact,—he
loves unworthily. In that which, of all things
in life, ought to have led him upwards, he
finds that which weighs him down. He himself disclaims the idea of placing the cause
here. Lucrezia, it is true, "does not understand nor care to understand about his art;"
but "Why do I need you?" he asks himself—

"——incentives come from the soul's self;
What wife had Rafael, or has Agnolo?"

And further Lucrezia had brought to him all

that he had demanded of her ; " the perfect
brow, the perfect eyes, the more than perfect
mouth, the low voice," were all his.   This he
had required of her ; this she gave him.   Why
blame Lucrezia?   He does not blame her.
And yet when, as on this night, the full
consciousness arises in him of what might
have been for him and his art, the regret will
come :—

> " Had you, with these the same, but brought a mind !
> Some women do so.   Had the mouth there urged
> ' God and the glory ! never care for gain.
> ' The present by the future, what is that ?
> ' Live for fame, side by side with Agnolo !
> ' Rafael is waiting : up to God, all three !' "

and he knows that the golden gates are
closed to him because he has linked his soul
to that which cannot enter in with him.

It was in vain that he tried to separate his
life into two distinct parts, his love on the
one hand, his soul's true striving on the other,
and to say,—" I will love unworthily, but I will
work worthily."   For, in the ordinary life of
every day, these two, which one may try to
keep apart, and which are indeed one, meet
and take hands, no matter how low the love,
no matter how high the work ; and how

much more true in this when a man's work
is art, which is all love, love operative on
things seen.   Carlyle has said :—" You may
see how a man would fight by the way in
which he sings ; " of Andrea del Sarto it
might be said,—" You may see how he paints
by the way in which he loves."   And this
is apart from the actual practical hindrances
that beset him.   Vasari tells us that he
was compelled to paint pictures that would
pay, not alone, as many an artist to-day
does, as pot-boilers, but to satisfy his wife ;
for the lovely face that looks out upon
us from more than one picture of the Madonna, veiled a spirit that was sordid and
grovelling ; the hand which holds the divine
child, that " soft hand," " a woman of itself,"
is the same that was held out to receive
the price of his betrayed art.   Browning
indicates this :—

> " I'll work for your friend's friend, never fear,
>   Treat his own subject after his own way,
>   Fix his own time, accept too his own price,
>   And shut the money into this small hand
>   When next it takes mine."

For, although he is doing inferior work, he is

working and working hard. One of the most touching points in Browning's sketch is the weariness of the man, joined to his conscious failure. He is spent in doing that which he knows to be of no true value. The irony of fate is shown in this, that he was exceptionally prolific in production. He has not failed from having let all his gifts lie fallow, like Aprile and Sordello; he has rather made the opposite mistake,—produced and produced abundantly. "Some good son paint my two hundred pictures—let him try!" he exclaims, with the only touch of bitterness in the whole, when he is reminded that he allowed his father and mother to die of want. To the reader there is a touch of infinite sadness in the cry; for, although the prostitution of genius is worse than the wasting of it, yet work is work; and the weariness of the worn-out worker appeals to the broad human instincts of us all, quite apart from the end aimed at. Yet it is true that, for Andrea del Sarto, his pictures will buy Lucrezia's smiles, and so he paints:—

> "While hand and eye and something of a heart
> Are left me, work's my ware, and what's it worth?
> I'll pay my fancy."

She shall have "the thirteen scudi for the ruff;" her cousin's debts shall be paid. But an influence in the wrong direction assuming a definite form like this, that could be seized and grappled with, was one that any man is able to combat; while who can fight against the air he breathes? The physical frame that can resist a blow or a sword-thrust, will succumb in the end to a subtle poison that daily, hourly creeps into the blood. Lucrezia created around her an atmosphere in which no high aspirations, no unselfish strivings could live, and this was the atmosphere that he breathed. And so his moral energies had gradually slackened; and little by little he had lost grip upon life and art. It was not the absence of incentive; it was the active deadening influence of her companionship.

And what he might have done and been, had his life been rounded off and complete, is not hidden from him :—

> "Had I been two, another and myself,
> Our head would have o'erlooked the world!"

Could he have said of love—

> "I'll take his hand and go with him
> To the deep wells of light,"

whither, one asks, might not that hand have
led him? Surely as far as the great throne
itself, whence all life springs, and round which
all life gathers. All this he knows and feels.
How he recalls that golden time at the French
court—

> "That Francis, that first time,
> And that long festal year at Fontainebleau!
> I surely then could sometimes leave the ground,
> Put on the glory, Rafael's daily wear,
> In that humane great monarch's golden look,—
> One finger in his beard or twisted curl
> Over his good mouth's mark that made the smile,
> One arm about my shoulder, round my neck,
> The jingle of his gold chain in my ear,
> I painting proudly with his breath on me,
> All his court round him, seeing with his eyes,
> Such frank French eyes, and such a fire of souls
> Profuse, my hand kept plying by those hearts."

But in the midst of all this the voice called
him,

> "— the low voice my soul hears, as a bird
> The fowler's pipe, and follows to the snare;"

and he put off the glory, followed and sinned.

And he is resigned. If, on this evening, he
does go back in imagination to what might
have been,—

> "Only let me sit
> The grey remainder of the evening out,
> Idle, you call it, and muse perfectly

> How I could paint, were I but back in France,
> One picture, just one more—the Virgin's face,
> Not yours this time!"—

it is as an idle fancy, no more. He knows that it is all far behind him, the die is irrevocably cast :—

> " 'Tis done and past; 'twas right, my instinct said ;
> Too live the life grew, golden and not grey,
> And I'm the weak-eyed bat no sun should tempt
> Out of the grange whose four walls make his world.
> How could it end in any other way?"

A kind of fatalistic mood possesses him this evening as he looks back upon the past :—

> " — the whole seems to fall into a shape
> As if I saw alike my work and self
> And all that I was born to be and do,
> A twilight piece. Love, we are in God's hand,
> How strange now looks the life he makes us lead ;
> So free we seem, so fettered fast we are !
> I feel he laid the fetter: let it lie !"

What moral opiate, one asks, has he been taking which has power to bind and deaden his spirit to this point?

And even after death there is still failure ; for at the parting of the ways that lead to light and to darkness, the angel with the flaming

N

sword that turned every way stands guarding
the way to the tree of life ; and the face is the
face of Lucrezia :—

> " Four great walls in the New Jerusalem,
>   Meted on each side by the angel's reed,
>   For Leonard, Rafael, Agnolo, and me
>   To cover— .   .   .   .   ."

but

> " still they overcome
> Because there's still Lucrezia."

CHRISTMAS EVE.

IN *Christmas Eve* Browning passes in review
three distinct developments of Christianity in
our own day; and has much to say on the
great question of Christianity itself in its
fundamental idea. There is an entire absence
of theological argument on any of the burning
questions which gather round this fundamental
idea, such as one would expect at first sight
on finding oneself carried from Zion Chapel
on the one hand to St. Peter's at Rome on
the other, and then again to the lecture-room of
a German sceptic. But, at the start, the speaker
of the monologue, who looks at the whole
subject from the standpoint of the Christian, in
telling us how he arrived at this standpoint,
brings us face to face with the stupendous
question,—did the Godhead take flesh?

A fitting introduction to the whole subject
is the passage in Section V. in which he
deals with the grounds of his own faith.
Here, while alone on the common with God
and nature, he worships God, apart, it is true,
from any Christian body, but as a Christian,
as one who believes in the God-man ; and
looking back, he reviews the different stages
through which his mind had passed before he
reached this point. His conviction is based
on the acceptance without question of two
facts,—the existence of God and the power
of God ; and in what follows it is to the
moral rather than to the intellectual argument
that the main appeal is made ; but although
the conclusion is not,—nor does it profess to
be,—logically argued out, it is nevertheless
thoroughly thought out in its intellectual as
well as in its moral bearings. Starting from
the assumption that God *is* and God *can*, he
arrives in the end, by a chain of thought to
him inevitable, at Christ.

Whether the speaker expresses the ideas of
Browning himself must remain more or less of
an open question. In a dramatic monologue one
must begin by assuming that the poet aims at

giving us the ideas and feelings of the character which he personates for the time ; but when we find the same ideas expressed more than once by widely different characters, the conclusion is not very far-fetched that here at least he is either deliberately expressing his own thoughts, or that unconsciously his own individual bent is showing through. Further, in *Christmas Eve*, the speaker is not a well-known character with well-known opinions. When Caliban or Don Juan speak, we feel bound to assume, if possible, that the monologue is dramatic in effect as well as in name; but here the speaker, a kind of floating entity, with no antecedents and no history, is committed by his past to no especial criticism of life and faith. The chief corner-stone in his structure, this argument from the power to the love of God, is at least a favourite one with Browning ; and it is not alone in *Christmas Eve* that the thought is carried one step further. The power of God, this fact, proves the love of God ; the love of God culminates, must culminate in Christ. This is very fully worked out in *Saul*. When once we admit the all-powerfulness of God we are face to face with this problem,—is God superior to us in all else, and shall the meanest of His creatures teach Him, be superior to Him in this one point, shall the creature love, the Creator not love?

"Do I find love so full in my nature, God's ultimate gift,
That I doubt his own love shall compete with it? Here the parts
    shift?
Here the creature surpass the Creator, the end what Began?"

This he finds impossible of belief. That man loves, this fact, is a proof to him that God must love infinitely. And does God love? Then God will surely do for his creature what even man, if he had the power, would do for his fellow-man, if he loved him. It is on this plea that David challenges the love of God to inter-fere on the behalf of Saul:—

"Would I fain in my impotent yearning do all for this man,
And dare doubt he alone shall not help him, who yet alone can?
Would it ever have entered my mind, the bare will, much less
    power,
To bestow on this Saul what I sang of, the marvellous dower
Of the life he was gifted and filled with? to make such a soul,
Such a body, and then such an earth for insphering the whole?
And doth it not enter my mind (as my warm tears attest)
These good things being given, to go on, and give one more, the
    best?
Ay, to save and redeem and restore him, maintain at the height

This perfection,—succeed with life's dayspring death's minute of
    night?

.   .   .   .

'Tis the weakness in strength that I cry for, my flesh that I seek
In the Godhead! I seek and I find it. O Saul, shall it be
A Face like my face that receives thee; a Man like to me,
Thou shalt love and be loved by for ever: a Hand like my hand
Shall throw open the gates of new life to thee! See the Christ
    stand!"

Karshish gives the converse when he, supposing
for the moment that God did take flesh and
dwell among us, deduces from this,—"So the
All-Great were the All-Loving too."

    Now, on this Christmas Eve, the speaker
tells us that his soul had long since brought
all to this single test :—

    "That he, the eternal First and Last,
      Who, in his power, had so surpassed
      All man conceives of what is might,—
      Whose wisdom, too, showed infinite,
      —Would prove as infinitely good;
      Would never (my soul understood),
      With power to work all love desires,
      Bestow e'en less than man requires;
      That he who endlessly was teaching,
      Above my spirit's utmost reaching,
      What love can do in the leaf or stone,
      (So that to master this alone,
      This done in the leaf or stone for me,
      I must go on learning endlessly)

> Would never need that I, in turn,
>   Should point him out defect unheeded,
> And show that God had yet to learn
>   What the meanest human creature needed,
> —Not life, to wit, for a few short years,
>   Tracking his way through doubts and fears,
> While the stupid earth on which I stay
>   Suffers no change, but passive adds
>   Its myriad years to myriads,
> Though I, he gave it to, decay,
> Seeing death come and choose about me,
> And my dearest ones depart without me.
> No : love which, on earth, amid all the shows of it,
>   Has ever been seen the sole good of life in it,
> The love ever growing · there, spite of the strife in it,
>   Shall arise, made perfect, from death's repose of it."

Human love calls out aloud for a God who loves ; and this love of God is found in Christ. This, the speaker tells us, he has long since decided for himself. The question is closed ; and in all that follows, his attitude is that of the Christian. When Christ appears to him, it is not as a stranger, but as one whom he has always known ; even his garment has "a hem he can recognise ; " when he speaks to him it is to say :—

> " Thou art the love of God,—above
>   His power didst hear me place his love,
>   And that was leaving the world for thee.
> Therefore thou must not turn from me,
>   As I had chosen the other part ! "

and again :—

> " I have looked to thee from the beginning,
> Straight up to thee through all the world."

He represents himself as estimating the worship at Zion Chapel and at St. Peter's justly only when in the shadow of the presence of Christ ; with him he can enter the professor's lecture-room ; while he holds to the garment of Christ he is right ; when he lets it go, he is wrong.

His classification of all those who, by any stretching of the term, can be called Christians ;—although to some of them he only grants the name in the indulgent spirit in which he would allow a child to think, when he rides a stick, that the stick carries him,—seems to be,—Catholics and not Catholics, the latter divided again into—those who look upon Christ as God, and those who look upon him as a mere man. This fairly well corresponds to the three classes given, if we remember that in each case the extreme type only is taken ;—Roman Catholicism, as the extremest development of Catholicism ; Zion Chapel community, in which all the most prominent

features of nonconformity are brought forward ;
the professor's lecture-room, in which the least
possible shred of honour is paid to Christ.
With not all Catholics does " the head swim ; "
not all nonconformist ministers are endowed
with " immense stupidity ; " not all those who
have honest doubts as to the divinity of
Christ have worn down the figure to the
mere shadow which is all that the " virgin-
minded " professor leaves us.   The Greek
Church ;   the Anglican Church ;   all   the
different developments of nonconformity ;   all
the finely graduated shades of doubt through
which we may pass, from the so-called broad
views of the mild agnostic, down to the attitude
of the professor, are passed over, and find no
special mention, because each may be placed
in one or other of the three classes.   It is
true that the special place of one or another
in the category is often a matter of keen
discussion, and possibly the line is not always
easy to draw ; but a line there is ; and the
extreme type seems to have been selected—
with doubtful justice, many of us may think—
as pointing the moral best.

We enter Zion Chapel first ; and here no

touch is spared that can call up before us a
vivid picture in which all the most repellent
features of nonconformity are brought forward.
We hear the creak of the door-hinge; we see
the splutter of "the single tallow candle in
the cracked square lantern;" we note the
congregation arrive one by one; "the fat
weary woman," "the many-tattered little old-
faced peaking sister-turned-mother," the
"female something," with lips too white and
cheeks too red, the "tall yellow man, like
the Penitent Thief," the "shoemaker's lad,
with wizened face in want of soap." All
this, with "the hot smell and the human
noises," unrelieved squalor and vulgarity, is
the setting which forms a background to all
the worst points in the system.

First there is the exclusiveness of the sect, in
virtue of which they, "taking God's word under
wise protection, correct its tendency to diffusive-
ness;" for although the little chapel rejoices
in the name of Mount Zion, to which, the
prophet tells us, "all flesh shall come," yet
there is "a something—a motion they style
the Call of them," without which none can
claim fellowship with them, and yet which

the world outside with its teeming millions
knows nothing of. The speaker sits an alien
among the elect. Next there is the overwhelming predominance of the personality of
the "preaching-man," who feeds his flock with
just that diet, and no other, which he has
found, or rather believes that he has found,
suitable to himself :—

> " —a patchwork of chapters and texts in severance,
> . . . .
>   Having clothed his own soul with, he'd fain see
>   equipped yours,
>   So tossed you again your Holy Scriptures."

Next, and as a result of this, there is the
distortion of the truth, not alone from misrepresentation, but from partial representation.
There is as much good as ill in the sermon ;
but even the very truths are false "in their
quaint presentment ; "

> "How could you know them, grown to double their size
>   In the natural fog of the good man's mind,
>   Like yonder spots of our roadside lamps,
>   Haloed about with the common's damps ? "

Thus, in his wholly arbitrary interpretation,
does he, "in fine irreverence . . . hug the

book of books to pieces." All this, however, might have been borne, had it not been for the complacency of the flock, none of whom seemed to find any fault with the spiritual diet supplied them. They sat on "divinely flustered," no one

> "Appeared to suspect that the preacher's labours
> Were help that the world could be saved without."

He flung out of the little chapel.

What a deep breath we draw when we find ourselves in the open again, and drink in deep draughts of the fresh, cool, night air! From the literary point of view this is one of the best passages in the poem. The change of subject is marked by a change in the form; and in the next section, the jolting, irregular metre and strange, almost grotesque rhymes have given place to a measure which is dignified and rhythmical, and a diction which rises higher in proportion as a higher note is struck. There is a lull in the storm; and we see the sky with its "ramparted cloud-prison" on the one side, while the "empty other half" seems in silence to know that the moon may appear at any time. "How this outside was

pure and different!" The speaker feels as if,
God speeding him, he was entering his church-
door now, nature leading him :—

> "——— Oh, let men keep their ways
> Of seeking thee in a narrow shrine—
> Be this my way ! And this is mine !"

In seeming confirmation of this choice is
vouchsafed to him there and then, to him, " one
out of a world of men, singled forth," the unique
and superb spectacle of the lunar rainbow. We,
who only read, are almost as much rapt in the
wonder of the sight as the speaker himself, so
masterly is the description, in its rugged
strength, its few rapid clear - cut strokes, and
its power of taking possession of one, a power
that clings to the words of one who sees.
Climbing the arch we soar upward,—upward,
until at last—

> "—— supreme the spectral creature lorded
> In a triumph of whitest white——"

We gaze with upturned eyes, "glutted with
glory," when all at once, sudden as a thunder-
bolt, there is a pause, a stop—

> "All at once I looked up with terror,
> He was there.
> He himself with his human air.

On the narrow pathway, just before.

．　．　．　．　．　．

I felt no terror ; no surprise ;
My mind filled with the cataract,
At one bound of the mighty fact.
' I remember, he did say
' Doubtless that, to this world's end,
' Where two or three should meet and pray,
' He would be in the midst, their friend ;
' Certainly he was there with them ! '
And my pulses leaped for joy
Of the golden thought without alloy,
That I saw his very vesture's hem."

But this is soon followed by " a fresh enhancing shiver of fear." Can Christ remain with him, with him who has despised his friends ? Every other question now recedes into the background ; he only knows—He was there, they are his friends, they love. The crust of outward circumstances falls off like a garment, and this one golden fact alone remains. Henceforth, fast holding to the vesture of Christ, he will follow whither he is led, nor shall he again be found to despise those who love him.

He next finds himself before St. Peter's at Rome, rapt in the wonder of the fabric :—

" Is it really on the earth,
This miraculous Dome of God ?

> Has the angel's measuring-rod
> Which numbered cubits, gem from gem,
> 'Twixt the gates of the new Jerusalem,
> Meted it out,—and what he meted,
> Have the sons of men completed?
> —Binding ever as he bade,
> Columns on the colonnade
> With arms wide open to embrace
> The entry of the human race
> To the breast of . . . what is it, yon building,
> Ablaze in front, all paint and gilding,
> With marble for brick, and stones of price
> For garniture of the edifice?"

It is the midnight mass of the Feast of the Nativity. Within the whole Basilica is alive:—

> "Men in the chancel, body, and nave,
> Men on the pillars' architrave,
> Men on the statues, men on the tombs,
> With popes and kings in their porphyry wombs."

We see the gorgeous ritual; we feel the thrill that runs through the immense concourse of people as the rapturous moment of "the main altar's consummation" approaches. "The taper-fires pant up," the incense suspires in clouds, the organ "holds his breath, . . . as if God's hushing finger grazed him," at the silver bell's tinkling,

> "Quick cold drops of terror sprinkling
> On sudden pavement strewed

With faces of the multitude,
Earth breaks up, time drops away,
In flows heaven with its new day
Of endless life, when He who trod,
Very man and very God,
This earth in weakness, shame and pain,
Dying the death whose signs remain
Up yonder on the accursed tree,—
Shall come again, no more to be
Of captivity the thrall,
But the one God, All in all,
King of kings, and Lord of lords,
As his servant John received the words,
'I died, and live for evermore!'"

And yet the ritual repels him. It seems to him to be the—

"——soul's too-much presuming
To turn the frankincense's fuming
And vapours of the candle starlike
Into the cloud her wings she buoys on."

He is experiencing the power that ritual possesses of repelling those to whom its true inwardness is a sealed book. He does not even dare to enter, so strongly does he believe that this is the intoxication of the senses. Further he believes that if from the summit of the fabric judgment were to drop her " damning plummet ", a fatal space would be shown between it and the founder's base.

O

But his experience on the breezy common under God's own heaven now stands him in good stead. He will not repeat the mistake that he has made in the chapel :—

> " I see the error,—but above
>   The scope of error, see the love."

And now comes over him in a great wave a sense of the love and devotion, the simplicity and the faith of those early Christian days ; when the Church, one with herself, cast her all at the feet of her one Lord :—

> " Oh love of those first Christian days !
>   —Fanned so soon into a blaze,
>   From the spark preserved by the trampled sect,
>   That the antique sovereign Intellect
>   Which then sat ruling in the world,
>   Like a change in dreams, was hurled
>   From the throne he reigned upon :
>   You looked up, and he was gone.
>   Gone, his glory of the pen !
>
>   .   .   .   .   .
>
>   Gone, his pride of sculptor, painter !
>
>   .   .   .   .   .
>
>   Gone, music too !
>
>   .   .   .   .   .
>
>   What ? with all Rome here, whence to levy
>   Such contribution to their appetite,
>   With men and women in a gorgeous bevy,
>   They take, as it were, a padlock, clap it tight
>   On their southern eyes, restrained from feeding

> On the glories of their ancient reading,
> On the beauties of their modern singing,
> On the wonders of the builder's bringing,
> On the majesties of Art around them,—
>   And all these loves, late struggling incessant,
> When faith has at last united and bound them,
>   They offer up to God for a present."

This passage, recalling as it does certain well-known stanzas in Arnold's *Obermann Once More*, while it has not the same classical ring, makes us realise even more forcibly—

> "————the wave
> Of love which set so deep and strong
> From Christ's then open grave;"

possibly for this reason, that whereas the love in Arnold's poem finds its power in the emptiness of life without it, the love here wells up strong and inevitable from the fountainhead of love itself. In the one, men, sick at heart, turned to the open grave of Christ from the extremity of their need; in the other, Christ is the one Lord of life for all.

With this quickened sense of the love which has built up the fabric, the giddy summit as well as the rock-firm base, the speaker is lifted into another plane. He who has still hesitated to enter even after he admits that

"their faith's heart beats," and that in spite of
the error truth is there, now yields to this last
test, which seems to him to be the supreme, the
all-important one. He cannot turn away
from—

> "So many species of one genus,
>   All with foreheads bearing *lover*
>   Written above the earnest eyes of them."

He only asks,—is Christ there? do they love?
Christ has entered ; he will enter too.

His tolerance is brought to the rudest test
of all when he finds himself next outside the
door of the lecture-hall of a college in some
old German university town. Here he listens
to the Christmas Eve discourse of the professor,
who, inquiring into the Christ-myth, leads his
hearers to the conclusion that, although the
story is, of course, wholly untrustworthy, "since
plainly no such life was liveable," and although
Christ was not what he asserted he was, or
what his followers, in their simplicity, said
he asserted he was, still, taking the popular
story as it stands, "when reason has strained
and abated it of foreign matter," it seems
clear that some man did live who gave rise
to the fable, and that he was "a right true

man,—whose work was well worthy a man's
endeavour;" and he recommends them to go
home, and to venerate and adore all that is
left of him. Surely Christ will not enter or
bid the speaker enter here. In Zion Chapel
or in St. Peter's the air may have been
poisoned; but this man was leaving no air
to poison. He cannot be required to enter
the exhausted air-bell of the critic. Besides
he challenges the consistency of the professor.
If Christ was only a mere man, why is he to
be worshipped? For his superior intellect?
for his superior goodness? Honoured? yes;
but worshipped? Can he be worshipped on
any other plea but that he differed in kind
and not merely in degree from other men?
Christ, so he judges, is not to be worshipped
because he was omniscient, while we only
know in part, or because he was perfectly
good, while the best of us sins. However
great his superiority in these two points
might have been, still he was nothing that
we are not *to a certain extent*. Take the
first,—his intellect. Why should this make
him an object of worship? since he has told
us nothing in the sphere of morality which

has not been told us also elsewhere, by manifold voices ;—

> " With this advantage that the stater
> Made nowise the important stumble
> Of adding, he, the sage and humble,
> Was also one with the Creator."

" Christ's goodness, then, does that fare
better ? " Was it self-acquired or the gift of
God ? Now, if the distinction between right
and wrong were wholly arbitrary ; if Christ
had invented goodness, as the alphabet was
invented ; and if he had given us the virtues
new, each with its proper name, the case
would have been different ; but the fact is
that what he has told us of right or wrong
is appraised by us only and when it finds an
answer in our own consciences. It is true
that he first brought to light virtues not
looked upon as virtues before, and that he
enlightens the conscience ; but the light does
not create the objects that it illumines. If,
on the other hand, his goodness came from
God, then he is as other men. Christians
will willingly rob Christ of the lesser glory
to crown him with the greater. His especial

work is not to make us know what is good, since—

> " —— the truth in God's breast
> Lies trace for trace upon ours impressed :
> Though he so bright and we so dim,
> We are made in his image to witness him— ; "

it is rather to enable us to do it. " 'Tis one thing to know, and another to practise," are the homely words in which Browning indicates this prime need of humanity. Light is indeed good ; but life is what we want ; and the true God-function is to give us the power to be that which conscience tells us we ought to be. This neither he who excels in intellect, nor he who excels in goodness,—neither the sage nor the saint, can do for us ; but only He who can say,—

> " Believe in me,
> " Who lived and died, yet essentially
> " Am Lord of Life."

and therefore we look

> " —— from the gift to the giver,
> And from the cistern to the river,
> And from the finite to infinity,
> And from man's dust to God's divinity."

But even into the professor's lecture-room

Christ goes; for the lecturer must have some
instinct that rises above his "loveless learning,"
since he exhorts his hearers to "go home and
venerate this myth;" and there is, after all,
a certain merit in his turning his attention
to the subject at all. The speaker has now
learned his lesson of tolerance. In his next
mood he reflects that there is no use in any
"further tracking and trying and testing." He
will cultivate "a value for religion's self, a
carelessness about the sects of it;" and practise "a mild indifferentism." "This tolerance
is a genial mood!" he is reflecting, when he
is rudely awakened from this pleasant sense
of repose by a renewal of the storm; and he
sees the vesture of Christ receding further and
further into the distance. Christ has left him.

Then he realises that it is those who are
indifferent who have no part or lot with
Christ; that for each there must be "one way,
our chief, best way of worship;" and that he
must strive to find it. He believes that—

> "—— God, by God's own ways occult,
>   May—doth, I will believe,—bring back
>   All wanderers to a single track;"

but that meantime he, the speaker, can only

know for himself. God, he believes, speaks
to each individual soul. What is a message
to one means nothing to another,—

> " Where one heard noise, and one saw flame,
> I only knew he named my name."

In the same way other men around him see
many things that are a blank to him; but—

> " — What boots it, while yon lucid way,
> Loaded with stars, divides the vault?"

And so he chooses.

It is remarkable that the plea for each
of the three classes reviewed that he puts
forward is in no case that which they themselves would have urged. The strongest
arguments in favour of nonconformity,—
the open Bible, the freedom of the individual, the so-called personal religion,—all
are passed over, and the worth of the system
is brought to the one test,—are they His
friends? do they love? In the same way the
claims of Catholicism,—the divine origin, the
witness of the ages, the inflexible clinging to
the faith once given, no matter how over-
larded it may be in some communions, the

P

continual refusal to take any one man's opinion as to truth,—all is ignored, and one plea towers above every other,—they love. Even with regard to the professor we find the same. All that can be said in favour of free-thought is ignored,—the honest search for the light, the struggle to be true to the intellect which no one but God has given us, the devotion to learning of this particular "sallow, virgin-minded studious martyr to mild enthusiasm," who is worn in body in the search after truth, having "kept his mind free from the fleshly taint." The chief plea put forward for him is that he does,—well, not love, but that he does admit that Christ was "a right true man":—

> "Oh, let me at lowest sympathise
> With the lurking drop of blood that lies
> In the desiccated brain's white roots,
> Without a throb for Christ's attributes,
> As the lecturer makes his special boast!
> If love's dead there, it has left a ghost."

It is for the sake of this "ghost" that the professor is tolerated.

That the choice in the end fall upon Zion Chapel is a foregone conclusion, and one in which no question of doctrine has any

part. He has just been . insisting upon this,
that God speaks to each individual soul singly
and that the prime duty of each man is to
read well "the sole book unsealed to him."
The Catholic, on the other hand, holds that the
book may be sealed or unsealed, but that it is
at best insufficient and untrustworthy ; that one
may be mistaken about a revelation to the
individual, coming, as it does, not directly, but
through the individuality, which is an uncertain
and varying quantity, affected by many extra-
neous circumstances, but not about a revelation
to a divinely-founded body which Christ has
promised to be with always. This is one of the
raisons d'être of the Catholic Church. If the
speaker rejects this principle, as many in whom
the individual light is exceptionally bright, and
for whom the starry way athwart the vault
is exceptionally lucid, are sometimes, for an
obvious reason, led to do, he must, of necessity,
if he chooses at all, choose Zion Chapel and not
St. Peter's at Rome ; and he chooses it, not for
that which it is, but for that which it is not.

Two points he is emphatic upon ; a man must
be tolerant, but he must not be indifferent ; he
must be quite sure for himself and not think

one way as good as another; and he must at
at the same time honour the feeblest spark of
truth in others. Even the professor is not
excluded from the circle of his wide-reaching
charity; although the blessing wherewith he
blesses him is certainly not what he, the
professor, would have chosen; for he prays
that, in the dusk of his life :—

> "When thicker and thicker the darkness fills
> The world through his misty spectacles,
> And he gropes for something more substantial
> Than a fable, a myth or personification,—
> May Christ do for him what no mere man shall,
> And stand confessed as the God of salvation!"

THE END.

William Byles & Sons, Printers, 129, Fleet Street, London, and Bradford.